THE LUNDØ CRUCIFIX

IN MEMORIAM
MOURITZ MACKEPRANG
POUL NØRLUND
HANNS SWARZENSKI

HARALD LANGBERG

THE LUNDØ CRUCIFIX

THE NATIONAL MUSEUM OF DENMARK

LUNDØKORSET

GRAND PALAIS · PARIS

31 · III. – 15 · VII. 1992

ALTES MUSEUM · BERLIN

1 · IX. – 15 · XI. 1992

COPENHAGEN · KØBENHAVN

1992

Bogen er udgivet i samarbejde med
Nationalmuseet, Forening for Boghåndværk og Dansk Kunsthistoriker Forening.
Oversættelse til engelsk af Jean Olsen.
Ny Carlsbergfondet og Konsul George Jorck og Hustru Emma Jorck's Fond
har ydet støtte til udgivelsen.
Publisher: Langbergs Forlag, Gråbrødretorv 3, 1154 Copenhagen K.
Bogen er trykt i Herning hos Poul Kristensen, kongelig hofleverandør.
Skrift: Abrams Venetian.
Reproduktionsarbejdet er udført af F. Hendriksens Eftf.
Papiret er 150 g Ikonorex Specialmatt
© Harald Langberg, printed in Denmark 1992
ISBN 87-88884-03-1

To all those who kindly advised and assisted me in the preparation of this book I extend my warm thanks.

De mange, der har bistået forfatteren under arbejdet og medvirket til at bogen har kunnet udgives, bringes herved en hjertelig tak.

H. L.

CONTENTS

INTRODUCTION

1. The Lundø crucifix.
Lundøkorset.

2. *Crucifix shown to the congregation on Good Friday. Gilded copy of the Lundø crucifix.*
Korset, som det fremholdes for menigheden Langfredag. Forgyldt kopi af Lundøkorset.

4. *The Cherub crucifix.*
Kerubkorset.

5. The Lundø crucifix. Engraving on the front.
Lundøkorset. Gravering på forsiden.

COPPER CRUCIFIXES IN DENMARK

The Lundø crucifix in the medieval collections at the Danish National Museum has probably been made in Denmark about 1140.[1]

It is of copper and has once been entirely gilded. Christ is shown with closed (or almost closed) eyes at the moment of death. »Father into thy hands I commend my spirit: and having said thus He gave up the ghost.« (Luke 23,46). The engraving above the drooping head of the Saviour reveals His spirit in the shape of a boy, assisted by two angels, being drawn heavenwards by the two hands of God.

Seen from the front, the four large, practically square terminals of the cross display frames hammered back from deeper central fields, once embellished by the symbols of the Evangelists but only two are now in place: the eagle of St. John above, and the ox of St. Luke below (fig. 1).

The central place on the reverse side of the cross is filled by a representation of St. Michael slaying the dragon. The saint, with shield and lance, thrusts his lance into the dragon's jaws in an act symbolising the triumph of God over the Devil (figs. 3 and 9).

The cross terminates below in the form of a spike (damaged), now hidden by the later addition of a copper knop and socket for fitting to a processional staff. The remaining upper end of the spike is c. 4 mm thick, whereas the rest of the cross consists of beaten sheet copper no more than 2 mm thick, although stiffened to some extent by inward turned chamfered edges. However, this was not sufficiently robust for a cross carried at processions in all weathers, and at some stage it broke and had to be reinforced with some large metal plates. Later on, probably during the Reformation in the 1530s, most of its gilding was scraped away. The plates were removed in 1945 when the cross underwent restoration, and the old gilding came to light beneath (fig. 3).

The chamfered borders framing Christ and the Evangelist symbols are richly decorated. The plaques of the two surviving symbols are executed in the same *repoussé* technique as the gilded copper plaques on our »golden altars«. They are attached to the terminals by rows of small triangular points or tacks cut in the copper of the cross, then pressed down over the edges of the plaques (figs. 1 and 11).

Curiously enough, the figure of Christ is hammered up from sheet copper which has the same high degree of purity as the cross.[2] Christ's arms are wrought in one piece, and affixed behind the chest in the same manner as that seen in several Danish crucifixes of wood (figs. 23-25).[3] Calves have been added to the legs to shape them, and a little closing plate seals the top of Christ's head. All the metalwork is strongly forged, nothing is soldered (fig. 10).

A crucifix entirely beaten out of sheet metal has not been a rarity. For instance, there is a similar though plainer example at the Danish National Museum, the so-called »Cherub crucifix«, presumably from the same period. It is also of copper but not of quite such pure copper as that of the Lundø crucifix[4] (fig. 4). The back of the Cherub crucifix figure is open (fig. 20), whereas that of the Lundø figure is closed by a thin copper plate attached in the same technique as the Evangelist plaques on the front (figs. 10, 14-16).

This would seem to suggest that both the cross and figure of the Lundø crucifix have been made by the same workshop. Not only is the copper of the cross and crucifix figure

6. *The Cherub crucifix, back. Scale 1:3.*
Kerubkorsets bagside gengivet i 1/3 størrelse.

the same, but the ornament on the cruciferous halo of Christ corresponds to one of the ornamental motifs on the front borders of the cross (fig. 10).

The Cherub crucifix, however, is slightly different. The length of the crucifix figure is such that a chalice engraved on the cross is hidden by the feet of the effigy (fig. 22). However, an analysis of impurities in the metal has established that the cross and figure are wrought of the same copper, possibly even from the same cast bar. This is of special interest because not only is there a certain amount to link the cross and the corpus of each crucifix with the other, even the engravings on the backs of both crosses have something in common.

As far as the crucifix figures are concerned, the Cherub crucifix displays Christ with raised head and level gaze as *Christus triumphans*, and the Lundø figure is *Christus patiens*,[5] yet there is a considerable similarity between the two in the rendering of details. For

18

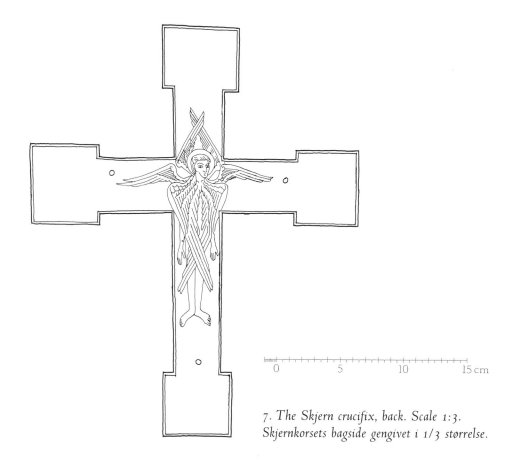

7. *The Skjern crucifix, back. Scale 1:3.*
Skjernkorsets bagside gengivet i 1/3 størrelse.

example, the loincloth's wide border and curious zigzag pattern at the sides – from the hips down (figs. 12-13, 14 and 20).

However, in terms of the cross rather than the corpus, the »Scanian« character of the Cherub cross has little to do with the more Continental form of the Lundø cross.[6] Nevertheless, Archangel Michael with four outspread wings on the latter, and the six-winged celestial being (often termed »cherub« in the Middle Ages) on the former are worth comparing (figs. 3, 6 and 9).

Cherubim and seraphim – strange elusive creatures – flutter here and there through the pages of the Holy Writ. Cherubim have four wings and seraphim six. Cherubim with unveiled hands often hover over wheels; in one source they are often described as having eyes on their wings.[7] In art they are treated as being of the same kind but simply given different names. On the casket of St. Pantaleon in Cologne the names CHERUBIN and SERAPhIN are inscribed above two figures, both have six wings with eyes on them, their hands are unveiled and they each stand above a wheel.[8]

A traditional depiction of this six-winged creature, though without a wheel, nor with eyes on the wings, is shown on a gilt-copper cross in Skjern Church, east of Viborg in Jutland.[9] The figure is most closely akin to a seraph, but probably meant to represent a cherub since it was the task of cherubim to guard Christ on the Cross. The Skjern figure is interesting in the present context because it is engraved in the middle of the cross, with one pair of stunted wings spreading to the arms of the cross, the others austerely folded, as if the engraver has found it difficult to articulate the motif (fig. 7).

The master of the Cherub crucifix, on the other hand, has arrived at a brilliant solution: the cross and cherub are perceived as a total composition. The vertical and horizontal lines of the cross merge with the spread of wings, and the figure seems to become at one with the cross. Certainly, it is rendered with such conviction that belief in the existence of this strange being is made imperative. There can be little doubt that this totality of effect has inspired the creator of the Lundø crucifix to give St. Michael an extra pair of wings spreading up the cross-arm above his head.

Technique and composition evidently link the Lundø crucifix with our other old copper crosses, and the same can be said of the connection between it and the golden altars. Not only are the two surviving plaques with Evangelist symbols on the terminals executed in *repoussé* in sheet copper like the gilded representations displayed on the altars; the small reliefs in the terminals of the Lundø crucifix are set in sunken square fields with decorated chamfered frames in the same manner as the altar reliefs. In addition, the Ascension of the spirit of Christ portrayed as a small boy, assisted heavenwards by two angels, is also seen on the altar frontal (now at the National Museum) from Sindbjerg Church north of Vejle in Jutland (figs. 18 and 19).[10]

The motif appears to have been very unusual. It is not known beyond the Danish frontier, and possibly it did not meet with the approval of theologists. In any event, the most feasible explanation for a rivet hole through the front of the Lundø crucifix must surely be that the engraving was once partly hidden by a riveted copper plate bearing the traditional inscription INRI.[11]

The Sindbjerg motif is of the same copper as the Cherub crucifix but contains fewer impurities, although it is not such pure copper as that of the Lundø crucifix, which is completely free of zinc and tin.[12] Copper of equal purity is used in the Broddetorp altar, as well as a reliquary from Eriksberg; both of these reached Statens historiska Museum in Stockholm from village churches in Västergötland.[13] Another reliquary of the same kind as the Eriksberg casket was acquired by the Skaraborg Länmuseum from Jäla in Västergötland in 1755.[14] All three have most likely come from Århus Cathedral, probably originally from the church consecrated to St. Clement, which was succeeded by the present cathedral in the Middle Ages (figs. 26-29).[15]

Reliefs hammered up from sheet gold, silver or copper are widespread, yet nothing is heard of figures *forged* in pure copper. On the other hand, some figures are recorded as being of pure – or virtually pure – copper, although nothing is said about the technique employed to make them.[16]

a.

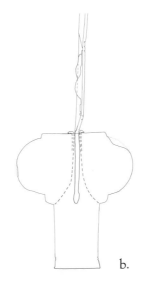
b.

8. *Knop and spike of the Lundø crucifix, a. from the front, b. from the side.*
Lundøkorset. Knap med tap, a. set forfra, b. fra siden.

9. Back of the Lundø crucifix. Scale 1:3.
Lundøkorsets bagside gengivet i 1/3 størrelse.

0   5   10   15 cm

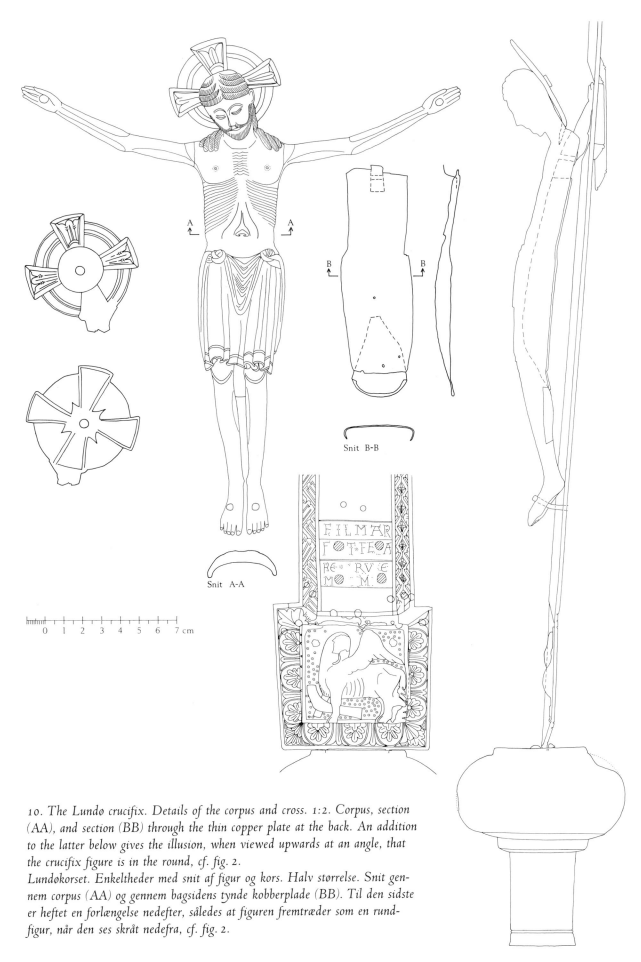

Snit B-B

Snit A-A

FILMÆR
FOTFEA
RE⚹RVE
MO⚹M⚹

0 1 2 3 4 5 6 7 cm

10. *The Lundø crucifix. Details of the corpus and cross. 1:2. Corpus, section (AA), and section (BB) through the thin copper plate at the back. An addition to the latter below gives the illusion, when viewed upwards at an angle, that the crucifix figure is in the round, cf. fig. 2.*

Lundøkorset. Enkeltheder med snit af figur og kors. Halv størrelse. Snit gennem corpus (AA) og gennem bagsidens tynde kobberplade (BB). Til den sidste er heftet en forlængelse nedefter, således at figuren fremtræder som en rundfigur, når den ses skråt nedefra, cf. fig. 2.

A EUROPEAN COMMUNITY

When the works of gilt-copper described here were created, Denmark belonged to a European community under the collective spiritual leadership of the Church of Rome. The King had formally affiliated his country to the Christian community about 960, and the big runestone at Jelling may be looked upon as a ceremonial proclamation, a document of ratification so to speak. In the twelfth century, the kingdom of Denmark was allotted its own archiepiscopal see in Lund, thus becoming a »full member« of the Community. As we have seen, there were firm links between Denmark and the ancient nucleus of countries, where great traditions had evolved through the centuries, also in the sphere of visual arts. Down to its smallest detail the Lundø crucifix bears this hallmark.

The Crucifixion has been the pre-eminent iconographical theme since the time of the Early Church, and representations of *Christus patiens* and *Christus triumphans* were conceived long before our two copper crucifixes were made.[17]

The circular nimbus to signify the radiance about the head of the crucified Son of God, and the heads of saints and martyrs, was already found in representations depicting the glory of Roman emperors in the days of imperial Rome.

The nimbus of the Saviour was soon given the mark of the Cross, and this form of halo was further enhanced by allowing the arms of the cross to project slightly beyond the circumference of the halo.[18] This latter type was employed in a Christ in Majesty miniature made at Trier 984/985, and in an ivory relief carved in Cologne about the year 1000 (fig. 31). Moreover, we see it frequently in the many works of bronze commissioned by Bishop Bernward the Holy between 992 and 1022 in Hildesheim, with which all who visited the renowned Cathedral School would have been familiar.[19]

The special type of halo spread to areas round Hildesheim. It is found in a magnificent Bible, »written, illuminated and bound« in 1094/1097 at Stavelot between Liège and Luxemburg (fig. 46).[20]

In the following century numerous examples appear in Denmark.[21] It is also found in the golden adornment of the Odder, Lisbjerg and Stadil altars, and the Broddetorp altar has a series of them (figs. 29, 32 and 23).[22]

Eskil, later Archbishop of Lund, like many young boys of noble birth in Denmark, had been sent (c. 1112) to study at the Cathedral School in Hildesheim. This special form of halo would have belonged to the impressions rooted in his childhood education.

Almost all the ornament on the Lundø crucifix occurs, together with the characteristic halo, in the Rhine and Meuse region, southern Belgium and the area round Hildesheim and nearby Goslar, seat of emperors at the foot of Rammelsberg in the Harz Mountains. And copper mines in the Rammelsberg district most likely supplied the copper which reached Jutland.[23]

The whole area was by no means an isolated enclave, but in close contact with the Roman Church, and the Crusades strengthened the old bond with Byzantium c. 1100.[24]

Certainly, Denmark's links with post-Conquest England (1066) were not as strong as in Anglo-Saxon times, whereas the pilgrim routes and religious houses of France attracted many travellers from Denmark.[25]

IMAGE OF GOD

It is written in the Old Testament that God created Man in his own image, therefore artists portrayed God as Man, and Christ his Son as »the Son of Man«. In Denmark no tradition existed for rendering the human body as art, but it did so elsewhere in the European community, particularly the regions once within the frontiers of the Roman Empire.

The delineation of a body with arms and legs as on the Jelling runestone could be easily accomplished, and we may suppose that carved figures in wood would have been equally simple, although in the case of Denmark this is pure conjecture because nothing has survived.

Within Charlemagne's empire efforts were made to revive the ancient standards of art, and much was achieved, including in Lower Saxony, the area which first became converted to Christianity under Charlemagne, and which was no great distance from the cathedral towns and monastic foundations which already existed. At least it would have been possible to collect patterns there, and details to imitate. Yet, it is impossible to say if anything, or indeed how much, was directly copied in Denmark.

All that was usually shown of God the Father was Manus Dei, the hand of God reaching down from empyrium. The Lundø crucifix is unusual in that Christ is assisted heavenwards by the two hands of God.

However, twelfth-century art centred above all on the Son of God. The Crucifixion posed the problem of portraying Christ with the bare upper torso, bare arms and legs of a man. The artistic rendering of this motif came from others in the beginning of the twelfth century. It would seem that Danish workshops gained their knowledge from the same areas which had inspired their use of the special form of cruciferous halo with projecting cross terminals. In fact it could be surmised, that this kind of easily comprehensible detail spread more easily, and that the more complicated skills such as proportions, movement and expression followed afterwards.

On the subject of details, it can be noted that the hair of Christ on the Lundø crucifix, centrally parted and falling in long coils on to the shoulders, is one detail often found in Lower Saxony, seen for example on the large bronze crucifix in Minden, a town south of Bremen, with which the Danish bishop of Schleswig was in contact in 1070.[26] This crucifix was probably cast in Hildesheim, where effigies cast before 1022 had this characteristic hair (fig. 30).[27]

The source of this detail remains an open question; it is found in St. Gallen books and far west in a Missal fragment dating from c. 1100, probably made in or near Tours and now in Paris (fig. 34).[28] The torso of Christ crucified on this fragment, as well as the Christ figure on the Minden crucifix share another very widespread detail: the nipple is encircled by a ring of dots. This little pattern is often used in Denmark where, in connection with the Odder retable, it has been described as being »embarrassingly true to nature« (fig. 33).[29] This is just a matter of opinion, although this particular »study from life« is unlikely to have been made in Jutland. In Germany, however, the motif continues to be usual far into the twelfth century. It is displayed by the Emperor on a costly piece of jewellery (armilla) for the upper arm.[30]

Why specifically this little pattern should have spread so widely is probably because

»the dotted circle« could easily be understood in relation to anatomical reality – also in Jutland. An accepted form of stylisation. Virtually the same can be said for several other »anatomical« details. For example, the way that muscular detail was shown in the outstretched arms of Christ on the Cross. Somewhere, at an early date, the muscles of the forearms were translated into lines extending from the wrist to the elbow with marked narrowing at the elbow. This characteristic probably became widespread because it conveyed an understandable physical detail, but already at the time of the eleventh century it evolved into an exaggerated, stylised shape which made the forearm seem to dominate the whole arm. The schematic principle continued well into the twelfth century, and can be observed on the corpus of a great number of crucifixes, including the Lundø and Cherub crucifixes.[31] At the same time the division between the upper and lower leg is marked by curious emphasis of the kneecap.[32]

The division between the right and left side of the chest might be shown by one or two dividing lines, and in the eleventh century the breastbone is marked by a series of small horizontal strokes. This last pattern became prevalent, sometimes continuing as far as the collarbone. On the Lundø crucifix these lines are fairly long and wavy, and seen not only on the effigy of Christ but also on the engraved Child (fig. 18).[33]

In the language of imagery these different descriptive modes may be compared with the set symbols which represent letters or ciphers. Illuminators at work on manuscripts in the scriptorium of a monastery learnt to use such signs. It went without saying that, when the above-mentioned anatomical details were depicted, ribs were also taken into account. The effigy of Christ on the Lundø crucifix has twenty ribs down each side of the sternum, and the engraved child is equally well endowed. Obviously, the scheme has been developed into a decorative motif, an ornament, whose symbolic value is dissociated from what is actually shown.[34]

The fleshy parts of the body between the chest and the loincloth were more difficult to render, with the exception of the navel which was virtually always shown, sometimes with great emphasis as on the Lundø crucifix. There are various models, seemingly more or less dependent on how the abdomen was perceived.[35] The perfect abdomens and superb bodies displayed in the art of classical antiquity did not leave their mark on early medieval art. Abdomens came in many versions, even those as round as the proverbial football.[36] However, the combination of round stomach and thin upper arms also occurs in life, seen of course nowadays on the beach, but in the early Middle Ages it was perhaps a sign of monastic seclusion and virtually no knowledge of athletes.

Certainly, when it is possible to discern some hint of classical inspiration in the contours of a torso, little more than the breast and navel are suggested.[37] More gently modelled abdomens are, naturally, more clearly shown by sculpture in the round, and the same might also be said of the early, pliant representations of Christ on the Cross.

In the illumination of books it is more difficult to capture this effect, but illuminators at workshops in Cologne and Trier seem to have succeeded in depicting rounded forms at an early date. On a crucifix in a Gospel book from Cologne, 996/1002, we see a »naturalistic« way of rendering arms and knees which seems to anticipate the line emphasis discussed in the above.[38] Even the round stomach is in evidence! Presumably a reflection of compositions giving generously rounded contours which recur of course in engravings. The pronounced arc above the loincloth of the engraved Child on the Lundø crucifix is known from book illuminations.

When shown on modelled figures some patterns are engraved, for example the nipples encircled by dots on the Lundø effigy are executed »in the negative«, impressed as they are in the smooth surface of the chest they can scarcely be termed naturalistic. But it should be remembered that all engraving was customarily finished with an inlay of brown varnish, like the Lundø crucifix would once have had, now unfortunately missing as a result of cleaning.[39]

Disregarding niggardly anatomical criticism, however, it seems feasible to conclude that these conspicuous lines and shapes were conceived in such mutual harmony that the whole work of art would have personified the suffering of Christ on the Cross, and given believers a sharpened sense of the magnitude of His sacrifice: to strengthen their faith and lift up their hearts.

THE LOINCLOTH

If man were created in the image of God the loincloth of God's Son had somehow to be envisaged. Scenes of the Crucifixion on ivory carvings dating from about 800 to 1000 reflect the classical conception of *homo nobilis*, but the loincloth is very variously depicted. Moreover, the classical tradition cultivated at the court of Charlemagne also held that the shape of the body be revealed by the garments worn, and this was largely followed in the rendering of variations on the loincloth.[40]

In the eleventh and twelfth centuries, when dependence on the artistic conceptions of classical antiquity had declined, the representations of Christ on the Cross still showed a variety of loincloths. Peter Bloch gives a good idea of the range in his classification of twelfth-century bronze crucifixes according to the type of loincloth.[41] The old notion of suggesting contours of the legs concealed by the loincloth recurs time and again, yet the treatment of the loincloth in it own right as an artistic detail is not neglected.

An obvious means of emphasising the legs is to allow the loincloth to fall in folds which taper towards the hem, as seen on the ivory relief believed to date to c. 1000, and thought to have been carved in Liège.[42] Something similar is seen on famous relics such as the Gero crucifix in Cologne from 969/976, and the bronze crucifix c. 1050 in Essen-Werden,[43] as well as the Frauenberg crucifix a century later, evidently made in Cologne c. 1150 (fig. 35).[44]

This kind of loincloth is depicted in illuminated manuscripts from the beginning of the eleventh century. It is seen in a St. Gallen manuscript probably with a Byzantine background,[45] as well as at Winchester in a schematic drawing made with compass and ruler in a Psalter c. 1070, but evidently not considered satisfactory (fig. 36).

The loincloth, with a character of its own, is an important element of an illumination with a strong Byzantine influence inserted at the back of the same book (fig. 38).[46]

None of these representations display the special relation between the lines of the loincloth and the linear modelling of the upper torso already described, and shown on the crucifix connected with works from Tours, probably painted c. 1100 (fig. 34).[47]

It is obvious that, at the beginning of the twelfth century, an effort has been made to balance the lines ruled in preparation for the loincloth with those for the naked torso, in order to achieve the necessary linear harmony between the two. This could be done in a number of ways, and the juxtaposition of pointed folds below the waist with the linear modelling above it was one of them, as shown in the French painting, and again on the Lundø crucifix, though here the abdomen is less pronounced.

To depict vestments with zigzag-like folds at the hem is much favoured in classical antiquity, and the manner continues for centuries in Christian art; many of the figures on the Danish golden altars are practically hidden by this form of drapery. The robe of Christ in Majesty on the Broddetorp altar, falling over one shoulder in these characteristic folds, is the correct version (fig. 29).[48]

A masterly Roman diptych from shortly before 400 shows it was understood at an early date, that this zigzag pattern gave conviction to the modelling of the body concealed by a garment. In this case, the drapery with the zigzag is thrust out to the side in a convincingly natural way (fig. 45).[49] On a relief at Salerno, probably from the close of the eleventh century, the detail is widely adopted; for example, down the side of the loincloth, although here not in harmony with the strangely curved chest and abdomen of the crucified figure. On the other hand, the fragment of illuminated manuscript associated with Tours shows the zigzag down each side of a virtually symmetrical loincloth.[50] Or, more correctly, almost symmetrical, because the loincloth is a little longer over one knee than the other. This is also seen on the Lundø crucifix (fig. 34).

The Tours figure has one leg slightly in front of the other, and more is seen of the leg behind, as here the loincloth is shorter due perhaps to the knot on this side of the extra cloth. This latter piece is paler than the loincloth under it, and folded as a V-shaped »apron« below the abdomen. This pale textile has zigzag folds down the sides, and before the knot on the left it resembles a belt (*cingulum*).

On the Lundø crucifix, Christ is shown wearing a loincloth knotted on each side at the waist, and behind the knots a belt is faintly discernible. However, it cannot be judged whether the loincloth and its V-shaped central fold are one and the same textile, or whether the »apron« and drapery at the sides are part of an extra cloth like the Tours example. The Lundø Christ is shown with one leg inclined slightly towards the other, and more of its knee is also visible. The triangular point seems to follow the movement of the leg as it were, while the torso is unquestionably frontal. The painter of the Tours figure accentuates the twist of Christ's body by drawing the abdomen and navel slightly off-centre, whereas the horizontal ridges of the breastbone lead obliquely in the opposite direction. The loincloths shown on both figures have decorated borders. The Lundø border follows the zigzag edges of the drapery on one side of the figure, and not on the other. It is not clear whether the same applies to the loincloth shown in the Tours painting.

On the figure of Christ from Carrizo in Spain, dated to the first half of the twelfth century, the decorated border not only follows the hem of the loincloth at the side, but also the edge of the central V-fold. A belt with the same pattern is clearly shown belting the folds of the loincloth at the waist (fig. 47).[51]

Finally, the zigzag edges of folds are variously shown on twelfth-century German crucifixes in New York and Berlin (fig. 41-42).[52]

A number of the many loincloths with a central V-fold from the waist have a knot at one side, viz. as in the Tours illumination; while others, for example the Winchester Psalter from c. 1070, are without a knot (fig. 36). Sometimes the loincloth is shown with a knot at each side of the waist, like the Lundø and Cherub crucifixes, also on the copper relief at the back of an evangelary called the Dalby Book in Copenhagen (fig. 44), a »Scanian« cross in Stockholm (fig. 40), and the Frauenberg crucifix (fig. 35).[53] A later, dated example of this version is shown on an engraving on a chandelier base plate executed 1165/ 1170 for Emperor Frederick I Barbarossa at Aachen.[54] Here, however, the knots no longer flank a clearly delineated triangle. The folds are translated into more semicircular contours, and the engraved figure of Christ in its entirety is significantly different to the Tours depiction dated (*very* approximately) to c. 1100.

Our Lundø and Cherub crucifixes are akin to the French crucifix on a number of points, yet, since there are also major differences, it is impossible to claim any direct link between the scriptorium responsible for the Tours illumination and the workshops which made our copper crucifixes. On the other hand, the sensitive, even poetic work of art from the area south-west of Paris, and the later, less emotive craftsmanship in copper crucifixes might have been inspired by a shared source, even though the crucifixes suggest more connection with areas lying between Paris and Denmark.

EVANGELIST SYMBOLS

The two surviving Evangelist symbols on the Lundø crucifix are, above, the eagle of St. John supporting a book, and, below, the ox of St. Luke with a scroll. The head of the ox is missing, but the hindquarters of the beast, and apparently its cloven hooves, indicate that it is indeed an ox (fig. 1).

Everything seems to show that these plaques in the terminals are in their original position. On most of the old crucifixes in Denmark St. John's eagle is above, and St. Luke's ox is often below.[55] Of more significance, according to Poul Nørlund, is whether the symbols hold a book or a scroll, in that Nørlund only rarely finds scrolls as part of these symbols before the twelfth century, whereas in the thirteenth century symbols with a book become the exception rather than the rule. The »golden altars« he divides on this basis into an »early« and a »later« group respectively, although he convinces himself that this division is wrong. On these criteria the Lisbjerg altar falls into the later, scroll group, and the Broddetorp altar into the early, book group. This Nørlund could not accept.[56]

The basis for drawing up the division is also weak. About 1000, the so-called »Gregory Master« of Trier made a Gospel book in which the first words of St. John's Gospel are framed by the four Evangelist symbols. The eagle is given a closed scroll, the angel a half-open inscribed scroll, while the lion and the ox each hold a book, or »codex« as it was called at the time (fig. 60).[57]

The illumination of Christ in Majesty in the Stavelot Bible from 1094/1197 shows a scroll allotted to the Evangelist symbols of angel and eagle, whereas the lion and the ox are once more displayed with a book (fig. 46).[58] The same sequence is given in the almost contemporary »extra« Crucifixion painting in the already mentioned Winchester Psalter (figs. 38 and 46).[59] In this light, then, it is hardly surprising that the eagle in the terminal of the Lundø crucifix holds a book, and the ox stands with a scroll. But why insist that one must preclude the other, when both forms existed concurrently? Moreover, it seems that their juxtaposition held special significance in the first half of the twelfth century. We will return to this discussion later.

Another problem touched upon by Nørlund is that it would be more straightforward to render the lion with a symbolic book held in its catlike paw, rather than in the case of the stiff-legged ox. Many artists have nonetheless shown the ox attempting to do so, although rarely with any success. There are examples of the motif on most of our golden altars, still other artists simply insert the book or scroll between the rigid legs of the ox, and this method is found among the later representations.

The Lundø ox is in a difficult position. A »paw« holding the scroll is discernible, but it may have been added later, replacing one of the ox's stiff legs. Unfortunately this part of the plaque is severely damaged, and a detailed examination of early photographs has failed to reveal precisely what it looked like before this. During repairs four holes were drilled through the plaque for the attachment of a large plate, thus virtually flattening the relief. In 1945 it was hammered up again by William Larsen, who also filled in the rivet hole where originally the ox's leg behind the scroll would have been (fig. 21). The ox symbol below on the Cherub crucifix, however, has from the beginning displayed not a cloven hoof, but a left front paw gripping the scroll (fig. 22).

Artists encounter difficulties when portraying winged creatures from the side, while at the same time attempting to create a total impression by fitting both wings into their motif. However, enough of the Lundø eagle's back wing is shown to give an entirely natural impression. The same solution is seen on a crucifix from Roskilde, but due to its very naturalness there is virtually no hope of dating or identifying the origins of this detail.

The small punched circles with a central point which decorate the background of both plaques are a very usual ornament in twelfth-century Denmark, yet, as far as I know, not nearly so widespread elsewhere. However, on the Continent circles with or without a central point do occur; for example, on a ewer for holy water from 1116/1119, on objects from Hildesheim, and on the Stavelot retable, c. 1150 in Paris.[60]

11. The Lundø crucifix. The eagle of St. John.
1:1.
Lundøkorset, Johannesørnen. Opmåling, fuld størrelse.

ST. MICHAEL AND THE DRAGON

Innumerable representations of the Archangel Michael are known from the eleventh and twelfth centuries. The account of the Last Judgement in the Revelation of St. John (12,7-13), with its description of the Archangel fighting the dragon, inspired many forms of art. Nothing is written in the Revelation as to the weapon carried by St. Michael, and in a number of paintings he is shown with a raised sword in his right hand, like the representation at Castel S. Angelo in Rome. We find the motif on the retable of the golden altar in Sahl Church, where the Archangel is shown standing inside a tower as a pendant to Abraham in the other tower, standing with knife raised to sacrifice Isaac.[61] Also in mural paintings from 1125/1150 in the churches of Hvorslev and Råsted St. Michael is portrayed with a sword.[62]

There are various ways in which the scene with a lance being thrust into the dragon's jaws is given. The Archangel might be shown grasping the lance with both hands as in the Byzantine-influenced monumental painting in Civate near Como, and in the Ratmann Missal from 1159 at Hildesheim.[63] In Denmark the representation is found on a granite relief in Starup Church, and below on the back of the gilded Onsbjerg crucifix.[64] In this last case the dragon twines sinuously at the foot of the cross, close to the earth fraught with evil until the day of redemption and destruction of the dragon.[65]

A noble rendering of the dragon's jaws can be given when the lance is held in one hand, and thrust straight down. It is a situation in which Christ is shown using the cross-staff like a lance, as in the engraving on the front cover of the Dalby Book (fig. 43).[66] An equally serene representation is given by an ivory carving c. 800, showing the smiling Archangel playing with a small dragon (fig. 48).[67]

The golden altar (Pala d'Oro) at Aachen has a far more dramatic representation, in which a militant Archangel drives the lance almost vertically into the enraged monster's jaws. The relief is thought to have been made in Fulda about 1020, and presumably donated to the illustrious Cathedral by the Emperor, who would certainly have approved of a scene showing a mortal battle between good and evil.[68] The reason why the lance is held almost straight must surely be due to the narrow confines of the scene (fig. 49).

Certainly, the round shield is evidence that this type of St. Michael representation in Aachen is related to another type, viz. the St. Michael engraved on the Lundø crucifix, but here the sloping lance seems to cut in a diagonal across the scene. This latter »scheme« was already circulating in western Europe; and in Denmark it continued to be used far into the thirteenth century in mural paintings. It has also served as model for the carved wooden effigies of St. Michael for the side altars in many Danish churches.[69]

The version which is of interest in the present context can be seen in a book made at Prüm, between Aachen and Trier, about 990/1000.[70] The similarities between this and the engraving on the back of the Lundø crucifix are many and cannot be purely coincidental (fig. 50). For instance the shield, the wings with small spread points of contour feathers, the figure's stance, and a detail such as the grip of the hand on the lance with a sharp bend of the wrist are displayed by both.

A related illumination is seen in a book written about 1125, at any event between 1107 and 1132 in the Cistercian foundation's mother abbey at Cîteaux, near Dijon in Burgundy (fig. 52).[71] Here, however, the wings are different, as well as the grip on the lance,

30

with hand under the shaft and thumb resting along it. This position of the hand has been employed earlier by Ingelardus at the monastery of Saint-Germain-de-Prés (fig. 51).[72] He has drawn the motif as an enrichment to a capital N, where the oblique downstroke merges with the diagonal lance to such an extent that the hand is partly concealed, although the thumb is visible.

In English books this is repeated in the letter M, where the whole lance and hand are visible.[73] For example, in a Canterbury Passional from 1100/1125, and a St. Augustine's manuscript from 1140/1160. In both cases the position of the hand is slightly imprecise, but closely resembling the French examples (figs. 54 and 55).

The detail of the bent wrist which we are able to follow from the Lundø crucifix south to Prüm, and from there down to the other side of the Alps to Lombardy, has disappeared on the way from France to England: this suggests that the engraver of the Lundø motif has not taken his model from the latter country.

In early medieval times the two principal centres of the St. Michael cult were Monte San Michele, north of Bari on the shores of the Adriatic Sea, and Mont-Saint-Michel on the Normandy coast. The route linking the two passed north-west of Milan through Ivrea, where in a monastery there is a painting of St. Michael which closely resembles the one from Prüm but *without a shield*. The small addition of a shield to representations of St. Michael, as J.J.G. Alexander has demonstrated, signalled the militancy of the German Empire. From there by some route came the round shield with radial lines as already depicted in the Prüm illumination (fig. 50), and which can be traced back to the days of Charlemagne (fig. 48).[74]

THE DRAGON'S HEAD AND TAIL

The dragon was the fabulous beast of myth and legend throughout the Germanic world before it entered the scene as the leading monster in medieval Christian art.[75]

When the teaching of the Revelation of St. John spread to northern Europe, someone must have surely appreciated the value of the familiar dragon as the embodiment of evil. A new threatening opponent against which battle could be made to illustrate the omnipotence of the Church, although the dragon with seven heads described in the Revelation has not been widely depicted.[76]

The earlier type with one head and a sinuous tail was the usual model; for example, like all the dragons shown in representations which follow the scheme we know from Prüm 990/1000, but with the exception of the dragon on the Lundø crucifix. While most of the other dragons have large decorative tufts at the ends of their tails, the tip of the Lundø dragon's tail, on the other hand, finishes with a head which is slightly smaller than the head into whose jaws the lance is thrust. It is highly conceivable that the idea of putting a head on a dragon's tail originated in Lombardy, as one inspired decorative innovation after the other spread from there to the rest of Europe. In Denmark in the twelfth century there were quite a number of representations showing a dragon with a head at the end of its tail, and Danish pilgrims would also have had the opportunity of seeing others on their journey south, for example in the crypt of the cathedral at Verdun.[77]

In archaeology the criteria of shape provide some guidance in relation to the heads of fabulous beasts, but the Lundø dragon is tricky because the head on its tail is the type with a short snout, whereas the primary head is more wolf-like. Both are equally common in Europe during the eleventh and twelfth centuries.

On the other hand, we have a small reliquary cross of Byzantine shape, with an engraving of the Crucifixion showing Christ with a bold dragon at His feet (fig. 78). The dragon raises its head, which has the same elongated shape and broad snout, as two dragon's heads at each end of the serpent-like chain which holds this pectoral cross in place. It is a Nordic dragon's head, archaeologically dated to 1050/1150. The cross, a find from an island called Orø in the Isefjord, Zealand, bears a Danish inscription including the words, »Olaf king«. The inscription must have been engraved about 1138/1141, but the plaque with the dragon (also the chain) may well be older. Under the plaque, and possibly even earlier than this, is the receptacle of poorer quality gold which contained the relic.[78]

Dragons and dragon's heads may have been inspired by the illuminations in manuscripts imported and copied, for example, by newly founded Danish monasteries in the twelfth century. Certainly, the books made round about in Europe at this period teemed with dragons and other fabulous beasts.

The monasteries in and around Cologne, Liège and Louvain produced many such books, and on their pages dragon's heads are often shown in the rich illumination of initial letters. Already in the first half of the eleventh century we find a capital L composed of serpentine ornament with the head of a beast at each end, and later on dragons were very often the sole motif employed for composing initial letters.[79] An A with a dragon painted in Cologne was copied c. 1123 at the Danish archiepiscopal see but honoured with a tail-head, not used on the Cologne dragon (fig. 59). These dragons sometimes intertwine so closely that it is difficult to discover where their heads and tails begin and end. Many of these strange beasts have several heads; sometimes dragons of this kind are shown on their own. The Premonstratensian monastery at Parc in Louvain produced a magnificent edition of the Bible in 1148, and a large ferocious dragon was used in it to form an extravagant S (fig. 58)[80]. The end of the tail is a man's head with open mouth.

The body and wings of this dragon are unlike those of the dragon on the Lundø crucifix, but both have the same double twist to their tails. Dragons following what we have termed »the Prüm scheme« often have this characteristic double or even triple twist, although the dragon depicted in the Prüm book is without. Nor does the dragon – of Lombardy ilk – shown on the Broddetorp altar have a double twist to its tail. This dragon is engraved on the mandorla (above right) which frames the relief of Christ in Majesty (fig. 29), and in many ways its markings have much in common otherwise with the engraved Lundø dragon. It should be pointed out, however, that the Broddetorp dragon has nothing at all to do with St. Michael and his lance.

This might support a hypothesis that, as far as dragons are concerned, the Prüm illumination of the 990s diverges from the mainstream of St. Michael representations which spread from Ivrea in Lombardy through Germany to Denmark.

Under a later abbot of Prüm called Ryotpertus, a Gospel book made before 1068 shows St. Michael standing on the dragon, and this dragon has a triple twist to its tail,

32

but its wings are entirely different. St. Michael, however, and the company of angels behind him have the same type of wings as the ones of which we know from the 990s. That the angels were depicted with St. Michael echoes the description in the Revelation of St. John (12,7), »there was war in heaven: Michael and his angels fought against the dragon; and the dragon fought and his angels« (fig. 56).[81]

SHIELD, HELMET AND MAIL

Whereas in the earlier versions of St. Michael holding a shield, he wears a costume which bears some resemblance to civil dress in classical antiquity, in the twelfth century he is equipped in a more military manner.

A south German book illumination made between 1175/1180 even shows the Archangel with helmet and coat of mail. Also with a different shield. For the little round Roman shield shown being held loosely in his left hand at the court of Charlemagne (fig. 57), and in a slightly larger format carried in a military fashion in both Prüm pictures, are replaced by a long shield, pointed below, of the Norman type.[82] The latter kind of shield had already been adopted in south German representations of soldier-saints like St. Gereon and St. Victor.[83]

The shield is richly represented in the Bayeux tapestry c. 1077, and this presumably explains why the term »Norman shield« applies to this shape of shield. In Germany soldier-saints are depicted with it at the time preparations were being made for the first crusade c. 1090.[84] Nevertheless, the origin of the shape is somewhat earlier. It can be seen in German book illuminations painted about 1030.[85]

At Cîteaux the Harding Bible, prepared under the guidance of Etienne Harding the Holy, has pictures where armies in battle are shown with pointed shields, and Goliath the giant appears with this kind of shield before he is felled by David. In the last volume of the Bible, at the beginning of the Revelation of St. John, (the Apocalypse), the Archangel Michael is depicted holding a »Norman shield«. He steps forward with sword in hand and chops off the head of a savage dragon. The composition is unusual in that Michael and the dragon form the first letter of the word »Apocalipsis« (fig. 53).[86]

In all drawings and paintings mentioned above with St. Michael, he is shown in half profile by skilled draughtsmen and painters. On the other hand, it cannot be claimed that the engraver of the Archangel on the Lundø crucifix has overcome the difficulty of this facial angle, in which one cheek is turned towards the observer, and the other is seen in profile.

The engraver follows the convention of showing small lines above and below the mouth, although for a small-scale engraving this is hardly necessary. He even includes a little arc for the projecting curve of the jaw, and two small vertical lines between the upper lip and nose to denote modelling there. The same details are more successfully portrayed on the crucifix figure of Christ. This line emphasis occurs in book illuminations.

In this context a Gospel book made in Cologne about 1140 should be mentioned, not only because the above facial detail is shown in a picture of St. Pantaleon, but more particularly because this saint wears a helmet of the same type as St. Michael's in the south German painting from 1175/1180 (fig. 57).[87] The same helmet can be seen on a sandstone sculpture of a soldier-saint from about 1090, which also displays the »Norman shield«, and chain mail.[88]

As far as the Lundø crucifix is concerned, St. Michael is without a helmet, his shield is of the round, Roman type, and his attire more close-fitting than is otherwise the case when he is shown in civil dress.

It could be conjectured that, as the south German representation of St. Michael is clad in mail, perhaps some form of corresponding protection would be concealed by the outer robe, or that the robe with (embroidered) checkered hem is an under garment »borrowed« from the *oeuvre* of Roger von Helmarshausen (fig. 9). In this context it is worth noting that the loincloth worn by the Christ corpus on the Lundø crucifix displays a border in a pattern often employed by Roger von Helmarshausen. Also he depicts the angel of St. Matthew with six wings, admittedly different in character to the wings of the Lundø St. Michael. In any event, it cannot be denied that the creator of the Lundø crucifix has in all likelihood been acquainted with the art of Helmarshausen, although the Evangelist symbols with magnificently rendered wings, which Roger displays on his renowned Trier book cover c. 1100, are based on biblical interpretation.[89]

The accoutrements of our Lundø St. Michael include a bag worn at the hip and shown in front of the leg turned towards us. A corresponding bag is shown in a Spanish ivory carving from the second half of the twelfth century.[90]

SUMPTUOUS BOOKS

One of the illuminations in the Stavelot Bible from 1094/1097, as already mentioned, represents Christ in Majesty flanked by the four symbols of the Evangelists; two of which display scrolls and two books. The wings and halo of the eagle of St. John (with a scroll) differ from those of the three other symbols; moreover, several artists have worked on the Bible. Its motifs have evidently been taken from various sources, and skilfully composed into a harmonious whole: none is subordinate to the other.[91] D.H. Turner has established that the Parc Bible from 1148 is typical of the *oeuvre* produced in the Meuse (Maas) area but, »it is not Mosan illumination at its most typical; there is considerable extraneous influence in it, and a number of hands at work. Some of the initials show German, Rheinish characteristics, and North French influence is particularly prominent throughout the book«. The dragon in the shape of an S is due to the French influence.[92]

Obviously, it is inconceivable that the monastic brotherhood should have converged on Meuse in order to demonstrate the excellence of their particular domicile. On the contrary, in this field the European communities learned from each other; and, in the mid twelfth century, for the common purpose of creating magnificent books, there seems even to have been a tendency to turn for collective inspiration to art of unrivalled excellence, old as well as new, from various regions.

The synthesis of sources and artistry resulted in the production of illuminated manuscripts of monumental splendour both in conception and in content. For centuries arcades were the architectural element chosen as a frame for the canonical tables. In some books, for example the Psalter from Munich (fig. 57), castle architecture is the backdrop of a scene, and it can sometimes be a little distracting, especially when the Nativity is set in a castle courtyard.[93]

Other paths, however, led to greatness, pomp and extravagance. In Ireland and Anglo-Saxon England much attention had been paid to the initial word of a holy text, and these insular characteristics spread to the Continent where they appeared in Reichenau and St. Gallen in the tenth century, and as added gloss to books of the eleventh and twelfth centuries.[94]

The opening sentence of the Gospel according to St. John, »In the beginning was the Word«, stirred the imagination of scribes and illuminators at an early date, and by about the year 1000 at the great abbey in Trier, which also produced books for the imperial family, a book was made where the Latin »IN« is seen to take the form of a large I intersecting a large N. This is the Gospel book from Trier by the »Gregory Master« mentioned earlier, in which the symbols of the Evangelists are depicted in the frame round the words »IN principio erat verbum«. These symbols are each placed in the middle of the square border, while at the centre of the illumination, at the intersecting point of the I and oblique stroke of the N, is the symbol Agnus Dei, undoubtedly a measure of deference to the imperial family, who had a special interest in precisely this symbol of the Saviour (fig. 60).[95]

The volume is the prototype of a Gospel book written in Cologne, and it has been copied in Echternach, where the influence of »insular« sources was very strong.

In the golden Gospel book (codex aureus) from Echternach, made about 1030, with the Trier exemplar c. 1000 as one of its models, the joining of I and N is repeated, but the Lamb omitted. The joined capitals are ornamented with golden vines, interlace patterns and animal-heads. All characteristics familiar in Anglo-Saxon books, where the customary position for Evangelist symbols has been at the corners of the border round the illumination, a detail repeated at Echternach c. 1030, although it occurs in fact a long time before on the Continent (fig. 61).[96]

We find in addition various forms of foliage and foliate vines inhabited by birds, deer, dogs, hunters and others. There were, thus, ample decorations to hand at the time many ornate Bibles were produced towards the close of the eleventh century.[97]

The creation of magnificent volumes continued. In the story of the Creation, moreover, the first word of the Bible, the Book of Genesis, begins »IN« (the beginning …). In the 1140s many hands were at work on the Parc Bible mentioned above, and with it, on one of the first pages the opportunity to enrich a monumental »IN« in the traditional manner with intricate motifs and ornament (fig. 62). Yet an entirely fresh element is at the focal point of these familiar intricacies, since at the intersection of the »I« with the oblique stroke of the »N« there is a representation of Christ in Majesty framed by a mandorla. Now, too, the borders of the picture are ornamented with scenes set in roundels, one at each corner, plus four roundels between these, i.e. one in the middle of each border. This is a feature seen on the golden altars from Jutland.

The illumination of the book included virtually everything: scenes from the Old and the New Testament, symbols, a profusion of tendrils and floral vines sprouted from the jaws of beasts, hunters preyed on birds and other wild life gathered in the luxuriant panels between the letters.[98]

St. Bernard the Cistercian abbot viewed the enrichments with displeasure, and about 1150 he forbade the Cistercians to paint ornate capital letters. Understandable perhaps, yet it cannot be denied, these glorious books harmonised closely with the belief that to give the holy writings a magnificent setting would bring God pleasure. This task was part of the Christian cult and it was principally carried out by the monasteries. The founding and endowment of monastic houses, as well as funding costly books, were seen to be votive offerings on the same level as the donation of churches and altars.[99]

Considered from this viewpoint scribes and patrons certainly deserved the reward of appearing in the pages of these books; or on their covers embellished as they were with ivory reliefs and gold plated mounts. The link through the centuries between book illumination and metalwork has been very tangible.[100] It goes without saying that the art of painter scribes has been informed by the craft of artists in metal – and the other way round.[101]

The artist-craftsmen capable of drawing designs for engravings and carvings would have undoubtedly possessed the skill to illustrate books, and might at any rate turn to them for inspiration.

And among all these people, there were some who took a lively interest in combining the many constituent elements into monumental works of art in gilded metal.

GOLDEN BOOKS AND GILDED METAL

As we have seen, medallions with symbols are depicted in the border illumination of initial letters prior to the twelfth century, and for generations the Dove of the Holy Ghost is shown above representations of Christ in Majesty. But to position Christ in Majesty in a mandorla at the centre of initial letters, with the Dove in a roundel in the border above, midway between the corner roundels, as shown in the Parc Bible, is a masterly stroke which did not pass unnoticed. It has been repeated on a number of our golden altars,[102] and there is clearly some connection between these and the Parc Bible. Yet, the latter is unlikely to have introduced the idea, in that three of the early golden altars display representations of Agnus Dei (albeit not the Dove) in the panel above. And this might suggest that the version with the Lamb has been known before the motif of the Dove was used on the altars.

There can be no doubt that the lamb symbolises the Saviour. In the Revelation of St. John it is explicitly written that the *Lamb* is the Lord of Lords and King of Kings. The evocation of kingship is a prominent part of this text. The Frankish rulers, from Charlemagne to Charles the Bald, wished to fill the role of the Saviour's chosen representatives on earth. They worshipped the Lamb, and on the Day of Judgement the power and the glory of their dominion would pass to Him. This is revealed in an imperial golden codex where the twenty-four kings of the Revelation offer their crowns to *the Lamb*.[103] It should be mentioned, in this context, that coins with Agnus Dei were struck in the reigns of certain kings, and that Eric Klipping (1259-1286) had a seal (evidently his privy seal) with Agnus Dei. Carved in a small hard signet stone it followed him to his grave in Viborg Cathedral (fig. 65-67).[104] At any rate, it cannot be purely fortuitous that Agnus Dei and not the Dove should be the symbol above the midpoint of three golden altars.

The Sindbjerg altar, one of the three altars (Lisbjerg, Ølst and Sindbjerg), is specially interesting because the scene showing the Spirit of Christ being assisted heavenwards is analogous with that on the Lundø crucifix (fig. 21 and 68).[105]

Most of the ornamentation and biblical motifs shown on the golden altars were employed over a long period of time, but it would be difficult to exclude the rest on the grounds that they were not! Nor in the twelfth century would there have been any special interest in where the origins of old material might lie. If any tendency emerges in the art of the 1140s, it is perhaps the desire to combine as many different elements as possible in compositions of monumental character.

At all events, this is how the creators of our golden altars seem to have approached their task. The tremendous range of different ornamentation, and the fact that there is not one bare patch on the Lisbjerg altar, for example, seems to bear out the supposition. When Nordic interlaced beasts, twining foliage from the South, geometrical figures, flowers and leaves intermix, while hunters prance past vines and mythical animals in the borders framing religious scenes, it must surely be in a conscious effort to reach some splendid goal (fig. 63-64).[106]

And in this they certainly succeeded. To talk of a primitive fear of space (*horror vacui*) is hardly applicable here. Extravagant golden ornament everywhere expresses the striving for a vision which in fact came about.

However, it cannot be denied that these manifold effects are difficult to muster as a means of dating the individual works of art. It is not the component parts, but their combination in the total composition which is crucial. The variety is controlled, held in the balance, with an eye to the final effect.

The three golden altars displaying Agnus Dei above the central zone are imbued with the same qualities so brilliantly expressed by the monumental, introductory illumination in the Parc Bible.

To return to the portrayals of St. Michael in the many monastic books which lead us to the Archangel engraved on the back of the Lundø crucifix, it is hard to ignore the possibility that the Ascension of the Spirit of Christ, engraved on the front, may stem from book illumination. On the Sindbjerg altar the ascent of the Spirit is combined with the Deposition.

In the Gospel of St. Luke it is written, »And when Jesus had cried with a loud voice, he said, Father into thy hands I commend my spirit: and having said thus he gave up the ghost«. (23,46). This is perhaps the principal context, and a motif in some lost illumination showing Christ expiring may be reproduced on the crucifix. But not originally in conjunction with the Deposition as on the Sindbjerg altar. Admittedly, a child is shown as the embodiment of the Spirit of Christ in the large Externstein relief, however the child is already safely in the bosom of God the Father while the Deposition takes place below.[107]

Unfortunately, the relief of the Deposition on the Sindbjerg frontal is very damaged, nevertheless another square relief on the frontal is in fairly good condition and lends itself for comparison with two sets of reliefs carved in morse ivory, possibly intended for fitting to the altar. These ivories have been executed in Cologne after 1150, and show the Ascension of Christ in a mandorla with the Apostles gazing up in wonderment. The Sindbjerg motif follows the same scheme, although it represents an earlier version than that used in Cologne with the banner of victory, etc.[108]

The Sindbjerg series of reliefs has probably been made about 1140, viz. plus or minus a decade or so. This dating also encompasses the distinctive representation of the Spirit of Christ Crucified on both the Sindbjerg altar and the Lundø crucifix. Indeed, in the case of the latter it signifies the dating of the crucifix as a whole, since the cross and the corpus are made as one. The crucifix exemplifies the exquisite care lavished on decoration and composition at this period.

The Tirstrup crucifix is of wood plated with decorated sheet copper in the manner of the Lisbjerg altar, and would seem to be contemporary with this altar. In 1926 Poul Nørlund dated both of them to about 1150; later on, Swarzenski and Peter Lasko suggested »about 1140«.[109] The gap is not wide, and if the last date is the more accurate then the Tirstrup and Lundø crucifixes are contemporaries. To which, of course, may be added the Cherub crucifix.

Even if the Tirstrup crucifix were an older wooden crucifix, it would have looked like new after adding gilded copper plating, gleaming like the other two crucifixes and its variety of decoration likewise picked out in brown or black. Works of art which differ greatly from each other it is true, but the same can be said about modern art today. Who hasn't noticed at an art exhibition where, say, the work of a dozen artists is represented, the vast difference between the *oeuvre* of one artist and the next?

The Tirstrup crucifix has been written about in enthusiastic terms, and rightly so, therefore nothing will be added here.[110]

Overlooked, on the other hand, seems to be the Lundø Master's skilful handling of ornament and marrying of diverse elements into a masterly composition. For example, the conviction with which the engraved motif of St. Michael fighting the dragon is incorporated in the cross, letting the Archangel's two pairs of wings and the tail of the dragon spread towards the four terminals with their enrichment of variegated plant ornament: a bouquet on the lower terminal, and rosettes on the other three (figs. 3 and 9).[111]

Turning to the front of the crucifix one cannot help but wonder at the outstanding delicacy of the Ascension of the Spirit of Christ. It forms a synthesis: the crucified figure of Christ, the incarnation; the engraving, the spirit.

The chamfered borders along the arms of the cross are decorated with three different types of ornament. These borders of ornament are juxtaposed so that a person looking towards the crucifix from one angle or another will always face three different ornaments. Certainly, the skill with which this crucifix is made, as well as the mastery of detail suggest the hand of an experienced artist-craftsman in metal (fig. 2).

Consider, then, the master of the Cherub crucifix, severely criticised nowadays, and possibly even in his own day.[112] His work is expressionist; less time is spent on details. He has hammered up the metal until the desired result is achieved. His figure of Christ brings to mind what Lionello Venturi has written about George Rouault: »His art takes us back through the centuries to the time when every picture on earth was a reflected expression of God.«[113]

ATLMAR * AILMAR * ALMAR

The inscription on the Lundø crucifix is found beneath the corpus and above the damaged spike (fig. 1, 2 and 10).[114]

It is not, strictly speaking, at one with the craftsmanship of the cross because the lettering is far more lightly incised in the copper than the rest of the engraved motifs and ornament. Four horizontal lines are scratched in the metal, and between these some dots and light strokes indicate the position of four or five rows of majuscules. However, this has probably simply been in preparation for added black or brown pigment, while the fact that more marks than necessary are seen on the third and fourth lines may well suggest that some trial lettering has been incised before the final choice was made.[115] There are similar preliminary engravings for painted ornament and letters on the golden altars.[116]

As we have seen, to complicate matters still further, sometime before the close of the Middle Ages, the inscription was mutilated by four rivet holes made for a reinforcing plate.[117] Traces of pigment might explain why the first word of the inscription was read as ATLMAR when the crucifix reached Copenhagen in 1874. Not until 1938, presumably after thorough cleaning did the name AILMAR (or EILMAR) emerge. But in neither case is it possible to identify the person behind the name.[118]

Two rivet holes disturb the second line so that only three majuscules T, P and E and one division mark are clearly denoted, the latter is composed of six dots encircling a seventh, and its position is between T and P. The third line seems to begin with a C turned into an R, apparently followed by an E, and a division mark like the first. With a little effort the last word on the line reads CRUCE; on the fourth line the initial letter, M, is doubtful. On the fifth line, faint – and doubtful – traces of a concluding letter A is all that can be discerned. (Not shown in the drawing fig. 10).

The amount of pricks suggests that they are stung as in the case, for example, of the Lisbjerg altar.[119] This is most distinct in the I and L on the first line, as well as the impressive T on the second line, but otherwise not easily discernible, although nothing would have prevented the painter from continuing freehand.

Several scholars have made a tentative reading as follows: AILMAR F(EC)T*PA(RA)/RE*CRUCE/M(DOMINI). In English, »Ailmar made prepare the cross (of the Lord?)«.[120]

Ailmarus or Almarus is an early French (?) Latinisation of a Germanic (German, Danish or Anglo-Saxon) name. It is used in the Domesday Book (1084/1086) by the Normans, and in medieval Danish sources.[121] The last two letters are normally omitted.

Ailmar accomplished a task, and no more than this is revealed by the fragmentary text. Certainly, the crucifix has been costly to make, but it could well have been commissioned for the oratory or chapel of some great man and his family. Moreover, the inscription may not have been added until the time the crucifix came to be bestowed on a church.[122]

For how long the crucifix had its place in Lundø Church is not known. Lundø was one of the small islands owned by the King in the Limfjord at the time Valdemar II the Victorious' cadastral roll was drawn up in 1231. At one time or other it passed to the chapter of Viborg; and, later, the church is described as »the chapel of Viborg Cathedral«.[123] It is conceivable that the crucifix came to Lundø from Viborg – in medieval times an important city with many churches and monasteries. However, ecclesiastical and monastic buildings, as well as their furnishings, underwent severe damage in Viborg during the Reformation, and already in 1529 it was decreed that all parish churches in Viborg were to be demolished.

Irrespective of the whereabouts of the crucifix during these upheavals, its gilding was presumably scraped off sometime in the course of the Reformation.

There can be little doubt that interest had long since been lost in preserving the inscription which recorded Ailmar's achievement. And as mentioned before, the four damaging rivet holes must date from the Middle Ages when the crucifix was used in processions.

The spike below had to be altered to enable the crucifix to be fitted into the knop before it was raised above the crowd as the sign of Christ, the conqueror of the world. The knop was perceived as the globe (orbis), corresponding to the ancient Roman globus imperialis, later to become the symbolic orb assumed by Western rulers: the pomum.

To hazard a guess at the original length of the spike is difficult, but this has probably been about 11/15 cm, the upper 3.5 cm narrowing slightly to make the spike seem like a taproot or lance point.[124] In practice it would have been fitted into a base to allow the crucifix to be placed on, or in front of, an altar.[125]

Yet the spike also held meaning as the symbolic link between the Cross and the sinful world, epitomised by Golgotha and its destiny since the triumph of the serpent, and the burial of Adam at this very place. Symbolised either by a serpent or a dragon, the power of evil was finally annihilated by the Crucifixion. There are pictures where artists have depicted Evil pierced by the Cross.[126]

On certain holy days the Crucifix would be held forth in remembrance of this, and the worshippers would kneel in prayer and kiss the feet of the Saviour (fig. 2).[127]

Ailmar was forgotten. In recent research, however, the question of his identity has stirred considerable interest.

When Denmark was liberated by the British army in 1945, and the collections of Danish museums were brought out of hiding, the decision was taken to send some of our finest art treasures to an international exhibition in London. The exhibits from Denmark included the Lundø crucifix, and the name Ailmar was mentioned in the catalogue.[128]

In England, Æthelmaer was well-known as the Anglo-Saxon form of the Latin name Ailmarus.[129] It was the name of a prominent Anglo-Saxon, related to the kings of Wessex, thought to have commissioned a reliquary, c. 1000, in the form of a silver cross, for a large fragment of the True Cross sent from Rome in 884 by Pope Marinus to King Alfred.[130]

The Lundø crucifix could not possibly be as old as this, but it had certain characteristics found in English work, which led to the conclusion that it was presumably English. In which case Ailmar had been an Englishman, and it was also suggested that the maker of the crucifix must have learnt something about his trade on the Continent.[131]

No-one can *prove* that this has not been the case; and, if so, one might imagine some connection with the Anglo-Saxon Æthelmaer cross, now in Brussels. It bears an inscription with words spoken by the True Cross in the visionary poem »The Dream of the

Rood«.[132] On the silver cross which served as reliquary are also the words: »Drahmal made me«.

Drahmal is hardly an English name. Some people have suggested that it might be Nordic, which raises the question whether Drahmal »who made« the cross may, after all, have been an Englishman of Scandinavian extraction.

CONCLUSION

Where Drahmal hails from remains a mystery. On the other hand, Æthelmaer, the person who evidently commissioned the Drahmal cross, grew up near the south-east coast of England, which at the time was regularly raided from abroad. The marauders were called Danes, and many of them probably indeed came from Denmark.

The archbishop of Bremen had been charged with the task of making the country truly Christian, and it might be imagined when Cnut of Denmark also became king of England, that he would have encouraged clergy to travel from there to his old kingdom for the same noble purpose.

However, it was not as simple as this. The archbishop even ordered the capture and imprisonment of one ecclesiastic journeying from England to Denmark. He was then forced to acknowledge the archbishop as his master in order to be released.[133]

Strangely enough, the names of the ecclesiastics sent from England were rarely native ones, thus it has been assumed that these emissaries of the Church had originally come to England from the Continent.[134] But perhaps this is a minor point. Dominions were as attractive to archbishops as they were to kings. The population was of less importance, at any rate to the princes of the Church. Nation states in the modern sense did not exist, and records show how surprisingly often clergy moved from one country to another, and monks to new monasteries subordinate to the mother institution.

It was essential for an archbishop to have well-trained people to send out into the world, and the see of Bremen was no exception.

Ekkardus (Esic), appointed bishop of Schleswig in 976, had grown up in Hildesheim and received a thorough education at the Cathedral School. He held the appointment in Schleswig until he died in 1026, but throughout his life his domicile was in Hildesheim, and he even became a canon there.[135] Bishop Bernward was a close friend. And, above all, Ekkardus would have experienced one of the architectural masterpieces of the west being built, viz. St. Michael's Church in Hildesheim, and seen the celebrated bronzes commissioned by Bernward.[136]

If it is correct that St. Michael's Church in Schleswig has been founded by Cnut the Great, it would be tempting to recall the link with Hildesheim, but unfortunately it is uncertain whether Bishop Ekkardus ever visited Schleswig.[137]

There is no metalwork enrichment dating from the time of Bernward in Danish churches, yet in the secular sphere there is evidence of artistry to equal the finest work produced in the empire to the south. A matrix excavated in Viborg, the venerable capital of Jutland in the Middle Ages, has proved to be the same as that used to produce the two magnificent disc-brooches of gold found in Hornelund, western Jutland fig. 73-74.[138]

Not until a later bishop of Schleswig, Ratolphus (c. 1045/1085), is it possible to trace a Danish connection in relation to sacred art executed in metal, and still in the treasury of a church, though not in Denmark. The cathedral at Minden burnt down in 1061, and when Bishop Ratolphus attended the re-consecration of the cathedral in 1071 he brought the gift of a reliquary, presumably identical with the silver-plated, house-shaped casket to this day in the cathedral treasury. One *repoussé* silver plaque shows the martyrdom of St. Peter. The church is consecrated to St. Peter (fig. 75).[139]

The provenance of the Minden reliquary is considered to be Hildesheim, yet as it so happens that St. Peter is the patron saint of Schleswig cathedral we will venture to put forward two hypotheses.

Firstly, that a similar treasure may have also been acquired for the last mentioned cathedral. And secondly, that a casket of this kind could have been made in Schleswig, particularly in view of the preparations that were initiated when the Archbishop of Bremen chose to hold an episcopal council in 1063 at the see of Schleswig.[140]

This is simply conjecture because no tangible evidence exists to corroborate either case, but suffice it to say that Jutland and, for that matter, the rest of Denmark were plundered time and again. During the Reformation the state undoubtedly robbed churches, monasteries, and cathedral treasuries of their plate and valuables with extra zeal.

The few ecclesiastical treasures of gold and silver to survive have almost all been found in the ground. Therefore our gilded metal enrichments to altars do not give a true picture of the costly objects which filled Danish churches in the early Middle Ages. Everything of value at that time has gone.

Some ornamental details on the Lundø crucifix are reminiscent of the art of goldsmiths, and it has plainly been a stroke of good fortune that the Lundø crucifix was executed in copper and that its thin plating of gold could easily be scraped off.

Gold and silver undoubtedly reached Denmark in large quantities in the Viking age, presumably some of it would have been used to embellish the churches built in great numbers in this country during the twelfth century. Perhaps a shortage of precious metals arose about 1140. This would explain to some extent the widespread use of copper, although unfortunately there is no firm evidence to corroborate the assumption. We know, however, that large payments were made by the treasury in the 1130s. In 1131 upon the murder of Cnut Lavard, Danish duke but also German vassal, the aged King Niels of Denmark was compelled to pay an enormous sum to the German King Lothar II to avoid war. But internal strife could not be avoided and the hostilities, which raged on until 1137 (mercenary horsemen were summoned), must have cost fortunes.

The turmoil subsided a little in 1137 when Eric III Lam was elected king, although in eastern Denmark peace did not come about until after King Olaf (mentioned above) was slain by Eric Lam's army in 1141.[141]

Eric Lam supported the Church, and in 1146 he retired to the monastery of St. Cnut's in Odense to become a monk. He died the same year and was buried in the monastery church.[142]

All in all the rule of Eric Lam between 1137 and 1146 favoured ecclesiastical life in Denmark. To begin with there was some difficulty over the appointment of bishops, but Eskil, bishop of Roskilde received the archbishopric of Lund. He took with him a gifted priest called Herman, who hailed from the vicinity of Aachen in western Germany. The latter was, in 1137, instrumental in bringing about the definitive rejection of the supremacy over the Nordic dioceses claimed by the archiepiscopal see of Bremen/Hamburg. Lund had secured its position as the metropolis of the North.[143]

An ever increasing number of churches and monasteries were built in Eric's reign; perhaps, as one enthusiastic chronicler claimed, a result of »the great abundance of riches« amassed in years of peace. Whether this was correct, and whether there were indeed ample supplies of precious metals cannot be substantiated.

Yet, the general picture of western Denmark at that time seems to confirm that about 1140 a large number of costly altar enrichments could very well have been produced in Jutland. And this part of the country continued to be at peace for some time before strife again broke out.

Little is known about Eric Lam. His mother was the daughter of Eric I Ejegod (»the kind-hearted«), and Eric Lam his grandson would have presumably been educated at the German courts like Eric I's son, Cnut Lavard.

Eric Lam married the daughter of a German margrave, and he must have moved in circles close to the imperial court. When his time came to be king, he surely felt it his duty to continue to give support to the Church as his grandfather had done. The status of the archbishopric established by Eric Ejegod was brought in order; Eric Lam bestowed generous gifts on Eskil, and the eastern part of Lund Cathedral had at last been completed and consecrated.[144]

In Odense where his grandfather had set wheels in motion for the canonisation of his brother, Cnut the Holy, and the enshrinement of his burial place, Eric Lam fulfilled long-standing promises to grant privileges and fresh sources of income to the monastery. He possibly also made changes to the reliquary which held the bones of St. Cnut.[145]

Testimony to King Eric's princely ideals is perhaps the fact that, like Charlemagne, he called himself David; and he may have appropriated the Agnus Dei as his emblem, perhaps his seal and standard. It would have given him the sobriquet Lam (»lamb«), like others who have been called after the device on their standard, helmet, signet, etc.[146]

It is noteworthy, though, that on three golden altars Agnus Dei is displayed above the central panel instead of the Dove of the Holy Ghost, and that these are the very three altars which date from the time of Eric Lam and the years immediately following his death. When Valdemar I ascended the Danish throne he did everything in his power to belittle Eric Lam and that branch of the family.

To pursue what has been written here about the reign of Eric Lam, it seems reasonable to divide into three groups the examples of ecclesiastical metalwork discussed in the preceding pages: a. Prior to 1137, b. From 1137 to the beginning of the 1150s, c. The concluding phase.

Among the earliest objects pre-dating 1137 are a chalice and paten found on the site of the Haraldsborg castle ruin near Roskilde, they must pre-date the destruction of the castle 1131/1132.[147] The superbly executed gilt-silver chalice and paten are probably representative of the period's costly church plate, long since destroyed (fig. 79). A carefully modelled chalice of the same type can be seen on one of the copper plaques from Tamdrup Church, although it casts little light on the dating of the plaque.[148] This plaque, like others with »historical« representations, could well have been inspired by a lost illuminated manuscript dealing with the baptism of the king of Denmark, probably Harald Blåtand (»bluetooth«). There were plans to canonise King Harald. The main idea was to commemorate the ordeal by fire of the missionary Poppo who converted the

King, or possibly to enhance the reputation of the archbishop behind the mission. A plaque shows the baptism with a foreign archbishop in a pallium officiating. This was unfortunate because the archbishop of Lund had received the pallium in 1138. The plaque was altered – presumably while being made – so that the bishop officiates without a pallium, which tells against a dating to the reign of Eric Lam (fig. 77).[149]

To the time of Eric III Lam (1137/1146) or about 1140, when Archbishop Eskil, who had studied in Hildesheim, and Herman from Aachen were two of the king's close advisers, we attribute besides the following: Copper-gilt plaques on the Åby crucifix.[150] Copper-gilt plaques on the Tirstrup crucifix.[151] Gilded plaques for St. Cnut's Church in Odense.[152] The Lisbjerg altar.[153] The Sindbjerg altar.[154] The Odder retable with crucifix.[155] Front and back plaques of the Orø crucifix.[156] The Skjern crucifix.[157] The Cherub crucifix.[158] The Lundø crucifix.[159]

Closely thereafter, viz. c. 1150, follow: The Broddetorp altar.[160] The Eriksberg casket.[161] The Jäla casket.[162] The Ølst frontal.[163]

In 1157 Jutland was made an independent kingdom for a short while. It lasted until 23. October of the same year when Valdemar I's army, south of the town of Viborg put an end to Eric Lam's successor, Svein III Grathe.

In gratitude to God for his victory Valdemar immediately founded Vitskøl Abbey on the shores of the Limfjord north of Viborg and Lundø. Denmark was once again united under one king.[164] The splendid plans for the abbey church of Vitskøl were implemented but never completed. The seat of power had been transferred to eastern Denmark.

The third, and in the present context, last group includes the three altar enrichments in Jutland which display the Dove of the Holy Ghost in a medallion above the representation of Christ in Majesty: The Sahl altar 1180/1200 ?[165] The Odder frontal c. 1200.[166] The Stadil frontal 1200/1220.[167]

Like all datings submitted in the absence of firm documentary evidence, the dates given here are based on assessment, and many well documented monuments abroad from the eleventh and twelfth centuries have had to be turned to in search of parallels. Nevertheless it is difficult to find satisfactory datings within the second quarter of the twelfth century, and to attribute material to precisely this period is fraught with uncertainty. Motifs are taken from a wide range of places. They are merged into total compositions of the type from which just a hint can be gleaned about the origins of our golden altars.

Possibly, too, in the present context, a contributory reason for the uncertainty attached to this very span of two and a half decades, might be explained by the changing approach to artistic composition emanating from the thriving centres of art in France, in their endeavour to create a world of imagery that was different in character to the imperial art of the Holy Roman Empire.[168]

The essence of total composition was form and image, unexplained in words: works of art experienced through the eyes of the beholder.

Therefore the question of dating the Danish art treasures, discussed in the preceding pages, seems to have been best answered by the assessments of scholars with a deep knowledge of European art in the eleventh and twelfth centuries. Obviously the last word on this subject has not been uttered, and it is the hope of the present writer that some of the illustrations published in this essay will help scholars further afield to shed fresh light on the problems.

Translated by Jean Olsen

44

LUNDØKORSET
og den jyske metalkunst i det 12. århundrede

I sommeren 1874 beså arkitekten og arkæologen Fritz Uldall den lille Lundø kirke ved Limfjorden. Som kender af middelalderlige metalarbejder måtte han hæfte sig ved et kobberkrucifix på alteret. Det havde været forgyldt, men den meste forgyldning var skrabet af, og korset var overhovedet i meget slet forfatning. Uldall så dog klart, at han stod over for et mesterværk i slægt med de gamle alterprydelser, der et halvt århundrede senere blev gjort almindeligt kendte af Poul Nørlund som Jyllands »gyldne altre«. Uldall skrev straks til sine foresatte i København derom, og brevet – af 9. juni 1874 – kom C. F. Herbst i hænde. Herbst var inspektør ved Museet for Nordiske Oldsager, der 1892 blev en del af vort nuværende Nationalmuseum. I Uldalls brev beskrives korset så indgående, at Herbst ikke var længe om at få det sikret for museet. Med en følgeskrivelse fra sognepræsten sendtes det 2. august 1874 til København (fig. 84)[170].

Efter modtagelsen indførte Herbst Lundøkorset i museets inventarprotokol som nr. D854. Om nogen istandsættelse endsige nøjere undersøgelse blev der foreløbig ikke tale.

Ved museets nyordning som et »Nationalmuseum« i flere afdelinger kom korset fra Lundø til 2. afdeling, hvor det placeredes i en opstilling gennemført 1892-95. Denne er nu kun kendt fra fotografier[171].

Det placeredes øverst i en vægmontre (nr. 208) i middelaldersamlingens første rum oven over et andet kors (inv.nr. D23/1982), som der er grund til at hæfte sig ved. Vigtige forhold binder de to kors sammen, uagtet de ved et første øjekast synes meget forskellige[172]. Vi kan ikke knytte noget kirkenavn til det sidstnævnte kors, men har valgt at kalde det Kerubkorset, fordi det på bagsiden har et indgraveret billede af en kerub, hvor korset fra Lundø har et billede af ærkeenglen Mikael.

De to højtstående himmelske væsener kommer fra samme skole, et fornemt sted, hvor man vidste, hvordan vinger skal spredes ud på dekorativ vis, når de præsenteres på den begrænsede plads, korsets form dikterer. Figurerne adskiller sig derved fra en mere traditionel bag på et kors i Skjern, som Uldall allerede henviser til i sit brev af 9. juni 1874. Skjernfiguren gør sig forgæves anstrengelser for at få vingepragten klemt ind i de givne rammer (fig. 6, 7 og 9)[173].

I montren fra 1890'erne var det kun forsiderne af de to kors man så, og her ville alle, der i sin tid betragtede korsene, sikkert hæfte sig mest ved de to Kristusfigurer, som har en del tilfælles. De var, hvad man kaldte »romanske«, med fødderne anbragt side om side. Havde fødderne været lagt over hinanden og fastgjort med en enkelt nagle, ville krucifikserne være kaldt »gotiske« og placeret i middelaldersamlingens næste rum[174]. Om nogen fodstøtte (»suppedaneum«) var der ikke tale. Med fire nagler gennem hænder og fødder var hver figur fæstet til korset.

Lundøkorsets Kristus har bøjet hoved og lukkede eller næsten lukkede øjne, medens Kerubkorsets ser ret frem for sig. Kun den sidste figur savner glorie, men en lille tap bag på hovedet viser, hvor den har siddet (fig. 20). Ingen af figurerne har båret krone.

Lændeklæderne minder om hinanden. Begge har de en karakteristisk trekantet fold fortil, kantborter forneden og et ejendommeligt zigzag-mønster fra hofterne og nedefter.

Helt forskellige er de to kors, hvortil figurerne blev naglet. Det flade Kerubkors er med sine runde korsender af en type velkendt fra Skåne[175], medens Lundøkorset har en vis lighed med det allerede nævnte Skjernkors, der dog som Kerubkorset er fladt. Lundøkorset er *ikke* fladt. Det gør sig netop bemærket ved en gennemarbejdet form og udsmykning, som allerede Uldall erklærede enestående i sin art og fandt beslægtet med de »gyldne altre«.

Man kan undre sig over, at Poul Nørlund kun periferisk nævnte Lundøkorset i sin store bog fra 1926 om disse altre, men grunden har formentlig været, at Lundøkorset var så medtaget, at en mere indgående behandling af det først kunne ske under og efter en restaurering, som bl.a. måtte omfatte fjernelsen af nogle klodset anbragte beslag, der dækkede partier, det måtte være vigtigt for Nørlund at se. I »Gyldne Altre« (s. 43) daterede Nørlund imidlertid Lundøkorset til »slutning af det 12. århundrede«, idet han gjorde det samtidigt med Broddetorpalteret i Stockholm og Sindbjergfrontalet i Nationalmuseet. Disse to arbejder daterer Nørlund (s. 205) med store forbehold til henholdsvis ca. 1175-1190 og ca. 1175-1200. I museets katalog fra 1938 sætter han korset til »C. 1175-1200«[176].

En restaurering fandt først sted 1945 i forbindelse med genopstillingen af middelaldersamlingen umiddelbart efter dennes delvise evakuering under krigen 1939-45. Arbejdet udførtes af konservator William Larsen, der har affattet en udførlig rapport, men Poul Nørlund fik ikke publiceret noget derom.

Nørlunds datering blev fastholdt, da krucifikset snart efter restaureringen blev udstillet i London. Kataloget fra 1948 (Victoria & Albert Mus.) siger »omkring 1175-1200«.

Endnu i Nationalmuseets 1949-katalog fastholdes Nørlunds datering, ca. 1175-1200, og han nåede ikke at gøre mere ved den sag. Poul Nørlund døde 1951, og først i 1954 påkaldte Lundøkorset sig igen almindelig interesse, da Charles Oman i Burlington Magazine publicerede sin artikel »An Eleventh-century English Cross«, hvor han daterer Lundøkorset til godt oppe i det 11. århundrede.

Uden at jeg her skal gå nærmere ind på Charles Omans argumentation, må jeg anføre hans bemærkning om forholdet til Broddetorpalteret: »Hvis der er nogen forbindelse mellem Lundøkorset og Broddetorpfrontalet, er det ikke som anskuet af Nørlund, eftersom det sidste arbejde må være et trekvart århundrede yngre. Det kan imidlertid være et senere produkt af den samme skole«[177].

Havde Poul Nørlund levet, ville han utvivlsomt have taget til genmæle, men ingen i Danmark sad nu inde med et kendskab som Nørlunds til europæiske metalarbejder fra middelalderen, og Omans opfattelse, som han 1962 gentog i en stort anlagt oversigt over engelske metalarbejder[178], blev taget til efterretning. Ja, man gik i Danmark endnu videre. I et katalog fra 1972 dateres korset til ca. 1025-75[179].

I 1984 blev Lundøkorset påny udstillet i London. I kataloget: English Romanesque Art 1966-1200 (nr. 229) dateres det til 1050-75.

Forinden det afsendtes, blev det opmålt af Torben Hjelm og røntgenfotograferet af Birthe Gottlieb, og der udførtes af konservator Peter Henrichsen en afstøbning, hvilket medførte, at det måtte skilles ad, sådan som det var blevet det i 1945, hvor William Larsen dog ikke løsnede selve korset fra den runde kugle, det var monteret i. Dette gjorde Peter Henrichsen, og alle enkeltheder blev gennemfotograferet. Samtidig iværksattes en undersøgelse med scanning-elektromikroskopi (SEM) og røntgen-mikroanalyse på Teknologisk Institut ved civilingeniør J.C. Balling Jensen, og dette materiale bearbejdedes i løbet af sommeren 1984. Hensigten var at skaffe et bedre dokumentationsmateriale til bestemmelse af korsets alder og placering i middelalderens kunsthistorie. De mange teorier, som i tidens løb var fremført om værksted og nationalitet m.v. savnede et sådant materiale som grundlag[180].

Det lykkedes imidlertid ikke at få alt samlet, før den ovennævnte London-udstilling blev åbnet 3. april 1984, og da var kataloget til endnu en London-udstilling under udarbejdelse (The Golden Age of Anglo-Saxon Art, British Museum).

Poul Nørlunds datering i 1926 – og den kunsthistoriske placering – var påvirket af datidens svensk-danske behandling af Broddetorpalterets forhold til Danmark. Den har imidlertid ikke været uimodsagt og bør nødvendigvis anskues nøjere, hvis forskellen mellem Nørlunds og Omans resultater skal forklares i dag. Endvidere må en række andre metalarbejder tages i betragtning. Det gælder først og fremmest Kerubkorset og Skjern-korset, som allerede i forrige århundrede blev holdt sammen med Lundøkorset. Men alt dette tager tid, og da det ikke kunne gøres færdigt, før den anden London-udstillings katalog blev trykt, fremkom nogle på disse sider meddelte, nye oplysninger desværre post festum, da de blev fremlagt på et symposium i London den 23. november 1984. Flere tilstedeværende ønskede dem publiceret, og et manuskript blev færdiggjort, men derved forblev det.

De nye oplysninger var måske også kun væsentlige for nogle få kunsthistorikere ude omkring.

Forgyldte metalkors er der talrige af uden for Danmarks grænser, og mange er udført af kobber; men er der hæftet en Kristusfigur på korset, meddeles det i reglen, at figuren er støbt i bronze. Om kobbersmedede figurer, som Lundøkorsets og Kerubkorsets, forlyder der intet, men det skyldes måske, at metalundersøgelser kun er udført i begrænset omfang[181].

På symposiet i London, hvor ikke blot engelske, men også franske og tyske kendere af middelalderens metalarbejder deltog, var der ingen der kunne nævne krucifikser svarende til de danske, der helt var udført som kobbersmedearbejder.

Efter at være vist tre gange i London skal Lundøkorset 1992 udstilles i Paris og Berlin.

Det er derfor fundet hensigtsmæssigt at trykke denne bog på et sprog, de fleste forstår, og forsyne den med et billedmateriale, der viser mere end det, der kan ses gennem en montres glas.

Kunstværker skal ses. Hvad der udtrykkes med former, linier, farver og guld opfattes gennem synsindtryk i et sprog, der er ligeså forskelligt fra det skrevne og det talte som musikkens og dansens. Der er derfor mange ude omkring, der gerne vil *se* middelalderens kunstværker og forsøge at opfatte dem i en større sammenhæng, for at få afklaret forestillingen om tidligere stadier i den europæiske kulturs historie. For sådanne menne-sker er det, der udtrykkes uden ord af de kirkelige kunstværker, af væsentlig betydning. Gode reproduktioner kan så være med til at fastholde indtryk eller åbne blikket for noget, de særligt interesserede gerne vil tage i betragtning. Der er derfor i denne bog lagt vægt på at få gode gengivelser publiceret, ganske som det for nogle år siden i bogen »Gunhildkorset« blev tilstræbt at få gode fotografier og opmålinger trykt. Bogen om Gunhildkorset fik sit store format, for at korset kunne blive gengivet i fuld størrelse. Noget tilsvarende er desværre ikke muligt for Lundøkorsets vedkommende.

Dertil er det for stort.

Ingen af vore gyldne alterprydelser er sikkert daterede. De kan kun tidsfæstes omtrent-ligt med henvisning til daterede arbejder uden for Danmarks grænser. Her er meget dog ikke så sikkert dateret, som man måske gerne vil tro. Nye undersøgelser fører som bekendt ofte til nye resultater, og meget er sket, siden Poul Nørlund skrev sin fremragende bog i 1926.

Et berømt billede af Maria med barnet, gengivet af Nørlund (s. 98), kan nævnes som eksempel. Nørlund siger, at billedet er udført mellem 1151 og 1173 med henvisning til C.F. Warner: Illum. Manuscripts (1903), medens D.H. Turner (1971) siger »circa 1130-1150«[182]. Den sene datering havde medvirket til, at Nørlund ikke ville sætte Lisbjergalteret tidligere end til ca. 1150«, medens Lasco i 1972 sagde »c. 1140«[183].

Dateringsforskelle på 5-10 år spiller i den forbindelse ingen større rolle, men betænkeligt bliver det, når det tilgængelige materiale i 1926 gjorde det muligt at anse en bogstavform på Sindbjerg alteret – det lukkede E – for først at forekomme efter 1175. Sindbjergalteret blev derfor sat til 1175-1200, uagtet det lukkede E optræder allerede i begyndelsen af århundredet[185]. En tilsvarende uklarhed herskede længe omkring brugen af N og n på Orøkorset. Anders Bæksted havde 1968 kaldt korsets inskription en »tilfældig indridsning« fra omkring 1100 med »det første n af normal majuskel- og det andet af uncial-type«. Det kritiseredes af Erik Moltke 1974 under henvisning til, at uncial-n-formen først »dukker op i slutningen af 1100-tallet, hvor den forekommer på Tikøb døbefont«. Den daterer Moltke ligeledes til 1175-1200[186].

Allerede 1972 havde E. Krüger imidlertid påvist, at den omstridte brug af forskellige n-former var anvendt i Danmark 1131-1146 under »forbrødringen« mellem Lund og det berømte kloster i Helmershausen[187].

For klarhedens skyld gengives her et billede fra 1148, hvor såvel det lukkede E som de to n-typer forekommer på rad og række. Det er hentet fra Parc-biblen, et af den europæiske bogkunsts hovedværker, udført i Parc-klosteret ved Louvain i Belgien (fig. 76)[188].

At nogle bogstavformer optræder tidligere end antaget kan naturligvis forekomme underordnet, men Nørlund holder Sindbjergalteret sammen med Tamdrupbillederne og karakteriserer dem som kendetegnet ved deres »dramatiske stil«[189] med »heftigt bevægede figurrige billedkompositioner, fængslende ved deres livfuldhed«. Når man betragter Sindbjergalterets korsnedtagelse med de mange figurer i aktion og sammenligner med korsfæstelsesscenen, der netop er afdækket i Tamdrup kirke, og som ikke kan være gjort længe efter 1120, og når man hæfter sig ved særtræk, der for Tamdruppladernes vedkommende peger mod 1140'erne, kan man ikke undlade at spørge, om det skulle være muligt i tiden omkring 1140'erne at finde løsningen på spørgsmålet om, hvem den dronning er, der står som stifter ved majestas-figurens højre hånd på Tamdruppladerne, medens en ukronet ungersvend(?) står på den anden side[190]. Tanken må falde på dronning Malfred, der var søster til Knud Lavards hustru og ægtede Erik Emune 1132, kun fem år før han blev dræbt. Manden over for hende kan da være stedsønnen Svend, der blev konge 1146. Desværre kendes hendes dødsår ikke, men har hun som enke været knyttet til Tamdrup, kan tavlen skyldes hende og være blevet til op mod 1146, d.v.s. i Erik Lams tid[191]. Netop da var det på trods af modstand fra ærkebispen i Hamburg-Bremen lykkedes den kyndige augustiner Herman, der kom fra omegnen af Aachen, at få Lunds stilling som ærkesæde for Norden fastslået. Ærkebisp Eskil havde sikret sig palliet i august 1138, og det kan måske forklare den rettelse, der er foretaget på Tamdrupbilledet af dåbsscenen, der upassende vistes med en *fremmed* ærkebisp, som bar palliet[192].

Det blev fjernet.

Om Erik Emunes stilling som magthaver falder begrebet »kejser« flere samtidige i munden[193]. Det har rimeligvis interesseret hans våbenfælle og efterfølger Erik Lam, der gør Ribes Domkirke til Erik Emunes gravkirke og selv anvender begrebet »majestæt«, som dengang skal have været forbeholdt kejsere. Titlen bragte dem nærmere det guddommelige – og pavestolen[194]. Følgelig måtte den være egnet til at skabe respekt for regenten. Ideen var, at konge og kirke sammen skulle stå for et velsignet »fredsherredømme«.

Erik Lam lod sig kalde David, som Karl den Store havde gjort det, og når der skulle diskuteres, om nogle jyske granitbilleder forestiller en dansk konge eller bibelens kong David kan svaret blive et »både – og«. Kongen har rimeligvis – som kejserne af det karolingiske hus – sat tilbedelsen af Kristus i Lammets skikkelse særlig højt. Ifølge Johannes Åbenbaring fremtrådte lammet som symbolet på herskeren over alt og udtrykkeligt som »kongernes konge« på den yderste dag[195].

Hermed rimer det, at den store sydportal fra begyndelsen af 1140'erne i Lunds domkirke – d.v.s. hovedindgangen for mænd under indvielsen 1145, hvori Erik Lam deltog – er prydet med et vældigt gudslam (fig. 80)[196].

Lammet indtager også en fremskudt plads på flere af de ældste gyldne altre, en plads som på de senere altre overtages af Helligåndsduen. Små medailloner med korslam dukker op, måske som modstykke til de spænder med »Jellingeløve«, Fritze Lindahl har opfattet som kongemærker (fig. 69-72). Det er tænkeligt, at den europæisk skolede Herman, der havde fået bispetitel og var blandt de prominente ved domkirkeindvielsen i 1145, har hjulpet kongen med det »imperiale«. Kongen var i al fald taknemmelig for Hermans tjenester og belønnede ham smukt[197].

Lisbjerg- og Ølst-altrene fik korslam af samme, ældre type – uden fanedug – som domkirkeportalens, medens der over majestasfiguren på Sindbjergalteret sattes et gudslam med fanedug. Det er muligt, at kong Erik havde gudslammet som felttegn i fanedugen og som personligt segl, »sekret«, sådan som Erik Klipping synes at have haft det. Tilnavnet »Lam« kan have haft med noget sådant at gøre[198].

Erik Lam var berømmet som kriger, men brugte som regent tilsyneladende alene sværdet for at sikre det fredsherredømme under kongens og kirkens fælles styrelse, som virkelig blev realiseret. Så trak han sig tilbage og endte sit liv som munk i Sct. Knuds kloster, hvor han blev bisat i kirken, der gemte hans morfars helgenkronede broders relikvier og således fik endnu en konges jordiske rester i varetægt[199].

Valdemar den Store synes at have brugt »dannebrogskors« som felttegn i fanedugen, og i hans tid som enehersker (1157-1182) har korslammet tilsyneladende ikke haft nogen fremskudt stilling[200].

Når det var tilfældet på Sindbjergalteret, kan det pege i retning af, at alteret er fra før Valdemarstiden. Af større betydning er det dog, at alterets relieffer typologisk må være tidligere end nogle billedserier fra Køln, meget omtrentligt dateret ca. 1150-75[201]. Bag disse billeder har man anet fransk indflydelse, og det samme har Nørlund gjort for Sindbjergalterets vedkommende, som han dog på grund af det lukkede E henførte til 1175-1200. Når dette argument bortfalder, kommer vi ned til omkring 1150, måske snarere lidt tidligere, d.v.s. til Erik Lams tid.

Medens alterets himmelfartsscene forekommer ældre end samme scene på Kølnerbillederne, er alterets gengivelse af Frelserens ånd, der bringes til himmels, rimeligvis en yngre version af Lundøkorsets. Det er en af grundene til, at korset i det foregående er sat til »omkring 1140«, idet en halv snes år mere eller mindre ikke bliver afgørende.

At den omtrentlige placering – ud fra et kunsthistorisk skøn – rammer tiden før Valdemarerne, må imidlertid tvinge til eftertanke.

49

Den europæiske baggrund for dette skøn er søgt vist i den engelske tekst, hvor danske arbejder, der er sat i relation til Lundøkorset, blot er henført til omkr. 1140. At forsøge noget mere detailleret nu, er ikke rimeligt. Poul Nørlunds ord fra 1926 om de jyske metalarbejder står stadig ved magt: »De angivne dateringer kan kun være skønsmæssige og tilnærmelsesvise, da der ikke er en historisk fastlagt dato for et eneste af stykkerne«[202].

Med træarbejder kan det forholde sig anderledes. Er der de fornødne årringe, kan træets fældningsår ofte bestemmes dendrokronologisk.

Nationalmuseets store kristusfigur fra Vellerup i Horns herred er sammensat af to træstykker, hvoraf det ene er benyttet til krop og hoved, medens begge arme er udskåret af det andet (fig. 23-25). Sammensætningen af træstykkerne kendes fra Åbykrucifiksets og Odderkrucifiksets trækærner, og den er - med kobber − benyttet ved konstruktionen af Lundøkorset (fig. 14-16). Det har følgelig været naturligt at søge figuren fra Vellerup dateret dendrokronologisk. Dette er så meget mere ønskeligt, som Francis Beckett − der ikke har bemærket denne tekniske detaille − finder, at Vellerupfigurens omhyggelige overfladebehandling ligesom Skullelevfigurens, ligeledes fra Horns herred, minder så stærkt om guldsmedearbejde, at man må spørge, om ikke en guldsmed har gjort begge arbejder[203].

Der blev i 1988 foretaget en grundig undersøgelse af Vellerupfigurens egetræ, og det lykkedes at få nogenlunde hold på 78 årringe, men det kunne ikke føre til nogen datering[204]. Heller ikke de to planker, der danner Sindbjergalterets bagklædning, har kunnet dateres dendrokronologisk, og da splintveddet synes fjernet fra såvel Vellerup-træet som Sindbjergtræet, er der ikke meget håb om at nå frem til blot nogenlunde præcise dateringer[205].

Men der er andre træarbejder, som måske kan hjælpe. Det er for nylig lykkedes at få alterforsatsen i Borbjerg kirke ved Holstebro dendrokronologisk dateret til 1250-1300[206].

Det giver håb.

Indtil videre må vi klare os med skøn, og det er formentlig tilstrækkeligt for de fleste.

Beckett daterede Vellerup- og Skuldelev-figurerne til 1150-1200 og talte om en guldsmed, hvis »stil i allersidste instans gik tilbage til fransk plastik« fra samme århundrede. Det gentages af Nørlund 1950[207].

Tror vi på historien om guldsmeden, kan vi godt drømme videre om dygtige mestre, som drog fra Jylland til Sjælland, da Valdemar havde sejret på Grathe hede og flyttede magtens centrum østover.

Så ser vi også gerne for os en rejselysten, som i sin ungdom havde vandret ad veje i det tyske, og været i Frankrig, ja måske i Tours, som vi har strejfet nogle gange i det foregående.

En europæer.

12-13. The right and left sides of the Lundø crucifix.
Lundøkorsets højre og venstre side.

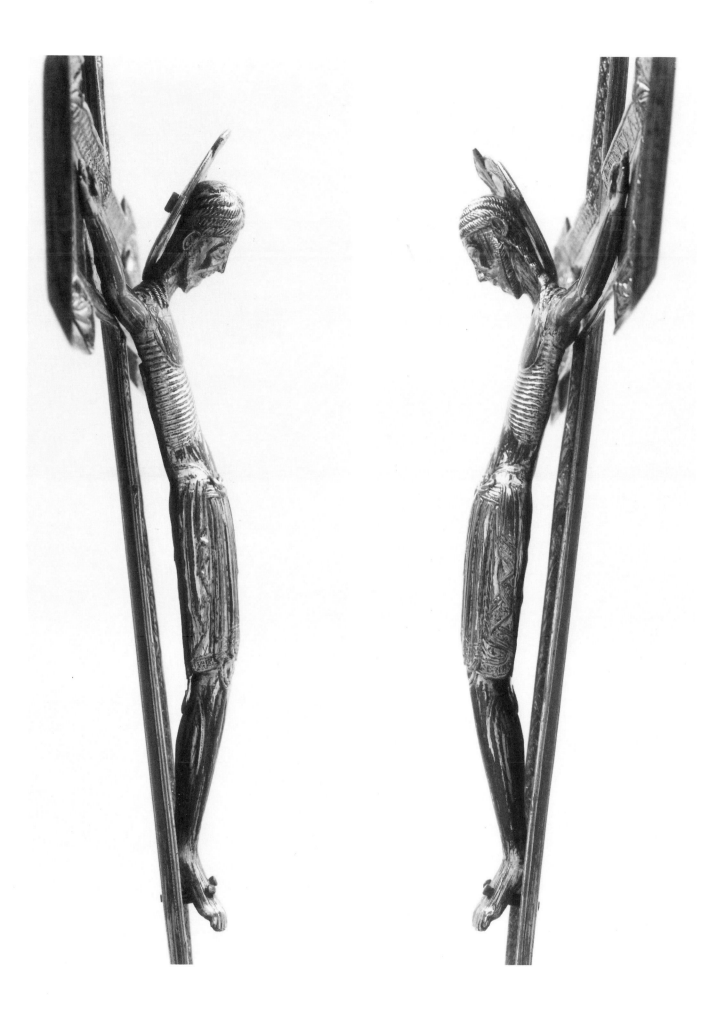

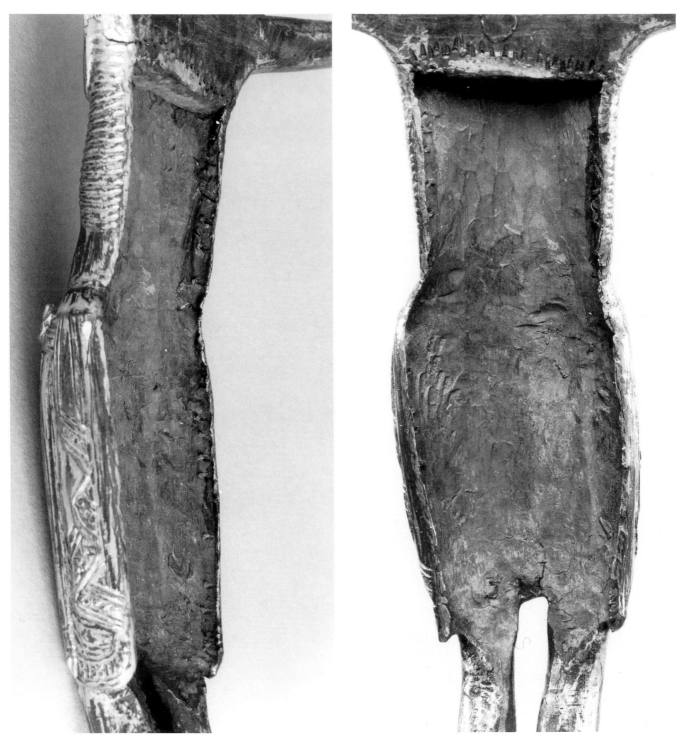

14-15. *The Lundø crucifix. The back of the corpus showing the zigzag pattern down the left edge of the loincloth.*
Lundøkorset. Figurens bagside med zig-zag mønster på lændeklædets venstre side.

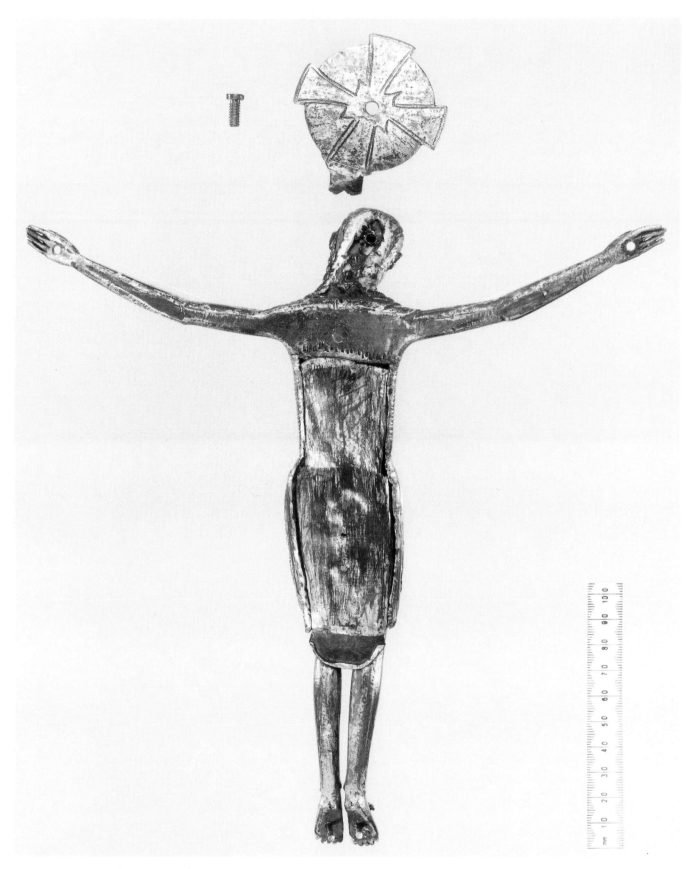

16. Back of the Lundø crucifix with cover.
Lundøkorsets bagside med dæksel.

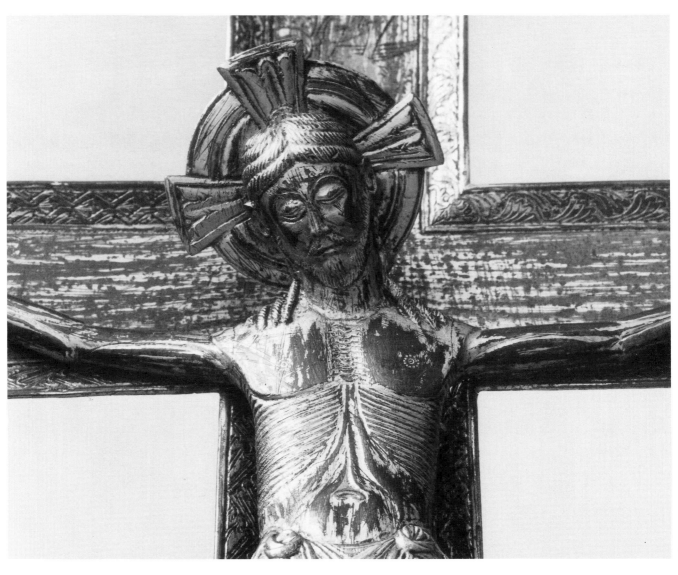

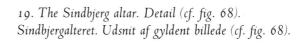

17-18. *The Lundø crucifix, head and engraving. Photograph 1945.*
Lundøkorset, hoved og gravering, fot. 1945.

19. *The Sindbjerg altar. Detail (cf. fig. 68).*
Sindbjergalteret. Udsnit af gyldent billede (cf. fig. 68).

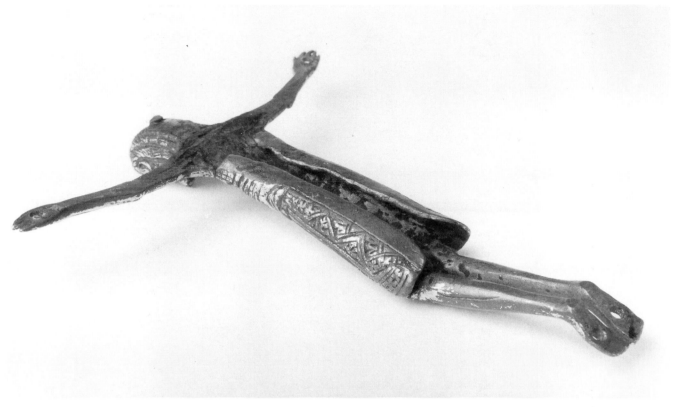

20. The Cherub crucifix. Back, with zigzag pattern down the left edge of the loincloth.
Kerubkorset bagfra, med zig-zag mønster på lændeklædets venstre side.

21-22. Lundø and Cherub crucifixes. The ox of St. Luke. Section of the Cherub crucifix showing rivet holes through the chalice normally hidden by the feet of the Christ figure (cf. fig. 4).
Lundøkorset og Kerubkorset, Lucasoksen. På udsnittet af Kerubkorset ses naglehullerne gennem den kalk, der normalt skjules af figurens fødder (cf. fig. 4).

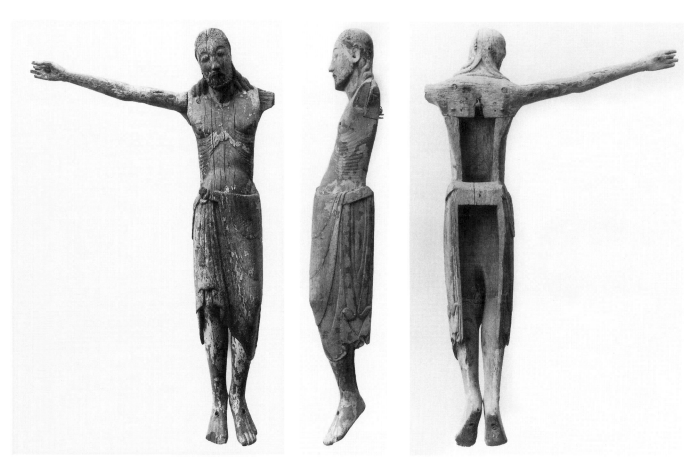

23-25. The Vellerup Christ. Copenhagen, Nationalmuseet.
Vellerup Kristus. Figuren set forfra, fra siden og bagfra.

26-28. The Eriksberg shrine. Stockholm, Statens historiska Museum.
Eriksbergskrinet fra tre sider.

29. The Broddetorp altar. Christ in Majesty. Stockholm, Statens historiska Museum.
Broddetorp alteret. Majestasfigur i mandorla.

30. Minden Cathedral. Figure of Christ. Schatzkammer des Mindener Domes, c. 1070 or c. 1100.
Minden domkirke. Kristusfigur, c. 1070 eller c. 1100.

31. Cruciferous halo. Ivory, c. 1000. Cologne, Schnütgen Museum (B 98).
Korsglorie, elfenben Køln ca. 1000

32. Cruciferous halo. Revninge, Funen. 11th century. Copenhagen, National-museet (D1444/1977).
Korsglorie fra Revninge på Fyn, 11. årh.

33. Cruciferous halo on the Odder re-table, c. 1140. Copenhagen, National-museet.
Korsglorie fra Odder retabel ca. 1140 (NM).

34. Crucifix painted in or near Tours (Maine or Touraine?), c. 1100. Paris, Bibliothèque Nationale, Latin 2659.
Krucifix malet i eller nær ved Tours (landskaberne Maine eller Touraine?), ca. 1100.

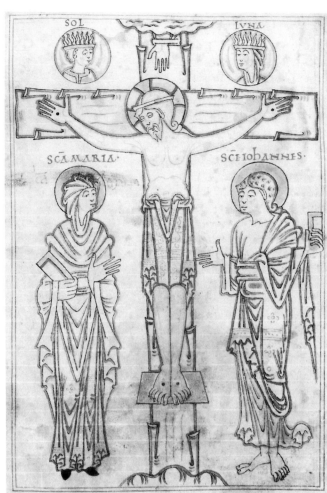

35. The Frauenberg crucifix.
Frauenberger Crucifixus. Figur i Sankt Georgs kirken i Frauenberg ved Köln.

36. Winchester Psalter. The Crucifixion, c. 1070. London, The British Library (MS Arundel 60).
Winchester tegning (ca. 1070).

37. Christ figure from Farhult, c. 1100. Lunds Universitets historiska Museum (inv. 3704).
Kristus figur fra Farhult, ca. 1100

38. *Winchester Psalter, The Crucifixion c. 1080?. London,*
The British Library (MS Arundel 60).
Winchester tegning, yngre end tegningen, fig. 36.

39. *The Ølst altar. Copenhagen, Nationalmuseet.*
Ølst-alteret, (NM, cf. note 163).

40. *»Scanian« cross from Ystad. Stockholm, Statens historiska*
Museum (23 002:75).
»Skånsk« kors fra Ystad.

45. Hygieia, ivory, Rome, c. 400. Liverpool, Merseyside County Museum.
Hygæa. Romersk elfenbensarbejde ca. 400.

46. The Stavelot Bible. Christ in Majesty, 1097. London. The British Library (Add. MS 28106 and 28107).
Stavelot bibelen, nu i London.

41-42. Christ Crucified. New York, The Metropolitan Museum (1.190.209). Gift of J. Pierpont Morgan.
Kristusfigur i New York.

43-44. The Dalby Book. Silver mount on the front cover, and gilt copper mount on the back cover, c. 1150?. Copenhagen, Kgl. Bibliotek (Ny kgl. Samling, 1325, 4°).
Dalby-bogen. Sølvplade på bindets forside og forgyldt kobberrelief på bagsiden, ca. 1150?.

47. Christ from Carrizo in Spain. Leon Museo de San Marcos, c. 1100/1150.
Kristus fra Carrizo i Spanien, ca. 1100/1150.

48. Ivory carving, Carolingian, about 800.
Leipzig. Museum des Kunsthandwerks.
Karolingisk elfenbensrelief, ca. 800.

49. Pala d'Oro in Aachen Cathedral. Relief, c. 1020.
Aachen. Guldalterforsats i domkirken. Relief c. 1020.

50. Prüm. Book illumination. Paris. Bibliothèque Nationale
(MS Latin 9448, fol. 71), c. 990/1000.
Bogbillede fra Prüm.

51. Book illumination from the monastery of Saint-Germain des
Prés, Paris. Bibliothèque Nationale (MS Latin 11683, fol. 4).
Bogbillede fra St. Germain-des-Prés klosteret i Paris.

52-53. *Book illuminations from Cîteaux. Dijon, Bibliothèque municipale, 1107-1132.*
Bogbilleder fra Cîteaux 1107-1132.

54-55. *Book illuminations from Canterbury. London, The British Library (MS Arundel 91, 1100/1125; and Royal MS I BXI, 1140/1160).*
Bogbilleder fra Canterbury 1100/1125 and 1140/1160.

56. *Prüm illumination from shortly before 1068. St. Michael leading the angels on the Day of Judgement. The right hand as in figs. 3. and 50. Manchester, John Rylands Library (MS 7, fol. 156 v). Prüm billede fra årene før 1068. Mikael som englenes anfører på dommedag. Højre hånd som på fig. 3 og 50.*

57. *St. Michael the warrior. Munich, Bayerische Staatsbibliothek (cod. lat. 27054,49 v). 1175/1180 Mikael som soldat. Sydtysk, 1175/80*

58. *The Parc Bible. Dragon with tail-head forms the initial S. (Brit. Libr. Add. MS. 14789, fol.83v) 1148. Dobbelthoved drage danner S i Parc-bibelen.*

59. *Dragon with tail-head in the initial A; painted in Lund about 1123. In Nekrologium Lundense, Lunds Universitetsbibliotek. Dobbelthoved drage i A, udført i Lund o. 1123.*

60. IN : Codex from Trier, c. 1000. Manchester, John Rylands University Library (Codex 98).
IN : Kodex fra Trier, ca. 1000.

61. *Echternach Codex. Nürnberg, Germanisches Nationalmuseum (Bibl. Hs. 156 142), c. 1030.*

62. *The Parc Bible. Design at the beginning of Genesis, 1148. London. The British Library. (Add. MSS 14788 f.6v), 1148.*
Park-bibelens indledning af Skabelsen, 1148.

63. *The Lisbjerg frontal. Copenhagen, Nationalmuseet.*
Lisbjerg frontalet (NM, cf. note 153).

64. *Varied ornament round the medallion with Agnus Dei on the Lisbjerg frontal.*
Lisbjerg frontalet, varieret ornamentik omkring medaljonen med Gudslammet.

65-67. *Eric Klipping's signet, centre (scale 1:1), between enlarged measured drawings of its engraving and its impression.*
Erik Klippings seglsten i midten (naturlig størrelse) mellem opmåling (forstørret) af stenens gravering og af et aftryk.

68. The Sindbjerg frontal, photographed before the medallion with Agnus Dei was stolen at the beginning of the present century.
Sindbjerg frontalet fotograferet før medaljonen med gudslam blev stjålet i begyndelsen af dette århundrede.

69-72. Two royal symbols with the Jelling lion, and two with Agnus Dei.
To »kongemærker« med »Jellingeløve« og to med Gudslam.

73-74. Disc brooch from Hornelund in western Jutland, and matrix for the base plate. Copenhagen, Nationalmuseet.
Guldbroche fra Hornelund i Vestjylland og matrisen, hvorover brochens bundplade er formet (NM, I 3866 og I 5353).

75. Minden. St. Peter's shrine, thought to have been donated to Minden Cathedral by the Bishop of Schleswig 1071.
Petersskrinet, som menes skænket Minden domkirke af Slesvigbispen 1071.

76. *The Parc Bible (cf. fig. 62). Illumination at the beginning of the Book of Daniel:* »*Anno tertio ...*«.
Parc-bibelen. Bogmaleri, med indledning til Daniels bog: »*Anno tertio ...*«. *1148.*

77. *Tamdrup. Relief. The baptism of the Danish king, Copenhagen, Nationalmuseet.*
Tamdrup-plade med »*kongens dåb*« *(NM).*

79. *The Haraldsborg treasure. Chalice and paten. Copenhagen, Nationalmuseet.*
Haraldsborgskattens kalk og disk (NM).

78. *The Orø crucifix. Copenhagen, Nationalmuseet.*
Orø korset (NM).

80. Cathedral of Lund. The south portal with Agnus Dei, c. 1140.
Lund Domkirke. Korslammets portal, ca. 1140.

NOTES *Noter*

List of the principal abbreviations
Vigtigste forkortelser

Alexander: J.J.G. Alexander: Norman Illumination at Mont St. Michel 966-1100, Oxford 1970.

Arb.: Nationalmuseets Arbejdsmark.

Beckett: Francis Beckett: Danmarks Kunst I (1924), II (1925).

Blindheim: Martin Blindheim, Nordisk Symposium for iconografiske studier 1976, 43-65.

Bloch: Peter Bloch: Staufische Bronzen: Die Bronzekruzifixe, *Staufer* V, 1977, 291ff.

Burl. Mag.: Burlington Magazine.

Bæksted: Anders Bæksted: Danske indskrifter, Kbh. 1968.

Cinthio: Erik Cinthio: Lunds Domkyrka under romansk tid, Lund 1957.

Cinthio 1958: Erik Cinthio: Majestas Domini Crucifixi, Meddelanden från Lunds Universitets historiska Museum 1958, 193-218.

Danefæ: Danefæ, red. af P.V. Glob, Kbh. 1980.

Danmarks NM: Danmarks Nationalmuseum, København 1957, cf. NMD.

DBhg: Danmarks Billedhuggerkunst, red. V. Thorlacius-Ussing, København 1950.

DGC: Danielle Gaborit-Chopin: Ivorie du Moyen Age, Fribourg 1978.

DK: Danmarks Kirker, udg. af Nationalmuseet.

DKm: Danske Kalkmalerier, red. Ulla Haastrup, Robert Egevang m.fl., 1985-87.

Engemann: Josef Engemann: Das Hauptportal der Hohnekirche in Soest, Münster 1991.

ERA: English Romanesque Art 1066-1200, Arts Council 1984.

Fests. HL: Strejflys over dansk Bygningskultur. Festskrift til Harald Langberg, Kbh. 1979.

Gauthier: Marie-Madeleine Gauthier: Emaux limousins champlevés etc., Paris 1950.

GB: HL: Gyldne Billeder, København 1979.

Gk: HL: Gunhildkorset, København 1982.

GLIM: Greek and Latin Illuminated Manuscripts, ed. M. Mackeprang m.fl., Kbh. 1921.

Grimme: Ernst Günther Grimme: Die Geschichte der abendländischen Buchmalerei, Köln 1980.

Guld i V.: Guld i Vestsjælland, København 1975.

Haussherr: Reiner Haussherr: Triumpfkreuzgruppen, *Staufer* V, 131-68.

Hildesh. D: Victor H. Elbern, Hans Reuther: Der Hildesheimer Domschatz, Hildesheim 1969.

Kahsnitz: Rainer Kahsnitz, Ursula Mende & Elisabeth Rücker: Das Goldene Evangelienbuch von Echternach, Frankfurt a.M., 1982.

Krüger: Ekkehard Krüger: Quellen zur Forschungen zur Hessischen Geschichte 21, 1972.

Lapière: Marie-Rose Lapière: La Lettre ornée dans Les Manuscripts Mosan d'origine Benedictine, Paris 1981.

Lasko: Peter Lasko: Ars Sacra 1200-1800. The Pelican History of Art 1972.

Liebgott: Niels-Knud Liebgott: Hellige Mænd og Kvinder, København 1982.

Lindahl: Fritze Lindahl: Dagmarkorset, Orø- og Roskildekorset, København 1980.

Mackeprang: M. Mackeprang: Jydske Granitportaler, 1948.

Marth: Regine Marth: Untersuchungen zu Romanischen Bronzekreuzen, 1988.

Merton: Afdolf Merton: Die Buchmalerei in St. Gallen, Leipzig 1912.

Minden: S. Kessemeier u. Jochum Luckhardt: Dom und Domschatz in Minden, 1982.

Nielsen: Lavritz Nielsen: Danmarks middelalderlige Haandskrifter, København 1937.

NM: Nationalmuseet, København.

NMD: The National Museum of Denmark, Copenhagen 1957, red. Aage Roussell.

Nyborg: Ebbe Nyborg: Mikaels-altre, Hikuin 3, Viborg 1977, 157-183.

Nørlund & Lind: Poul Nørlund og Egm. Lind: Danmarks romanske Kalkmalerier, Peintures romanes des eglises de Danemark, Kbh. 1944.

Nørlund GA: Poul Nørlund: Gyldne Altre. Danish Metal work from the Romanesque Period, Kbh. 1926.

OE: Ornamenta Ecclesia, 1-3, Køln 1985.

Oldeberg: Andreas Oldeberg: Metallteknik under Vikingatid och Medeltid, Stockholm 1966.

Oman: Charles Oman: An Eleventh-Century English Cross, *Burl. Mag.* 1954.

Oursel Cit.: C. Oursel: La Miniature du XII siècle a L'Abbaye de Citeaux, Dijon 1926.

Oursel Rév.: Raymond Oursel: Révelation de la peinture romane, 1980.

RiM: D.H. Turner: Romanesque illuminated Manuscripts, London 1971.

RO: X. Barral i Altet, F. Avril & D. Gaborit-Chopin: Les Royaumes d'Occident, UdF Paris 1983.

Rom. St. Romanske Stenarbejder 1 (1981), 2 (1984), red. af Jens Vellev.

Romanik: UdK, Romanik I-II. Tysk oversættelse af RO, München 1983.

RuM: Rhein und Maas, Kunst und Kultur, I-II, Köln 1972.

Schiller: Gertrud Schiller: Iconografie.

Schlesw. Dom: 850 Jahre St.-Petri-Dom zu Schleswig, Schleswig 1984.

SfV: Skatte f. Valdemar Sejrs tid, udstillingskat., Viborg 1991.

Skyum-N: Niels Skyum-Nielsen: Kvinde og slave, Kbh. 1971.

Springer: Peter Springer: Kreuzfüsse, 1981.

Staufer: Die Zeit der Staufer, Udstillingskatalog I-IV, Stuttgart 1977, V 1979.

Steenbock: Frauke Steenbock: Der kirchliche Prachteinband im frühen Mittelalter, Berlin 1965.

Steenstrup: Johannes Steenstrup: Normannerne I-IV, København 1976-82/1972.

Swarzenski: Hanns Swarzenski: Monuments of Romanesque Art, London 1954.

Tamdrup k.: Ole Schiørring (red.): Tamdrup kirke og gård, 1991.

The Golden Age: The Golden Age of Anglo-Saxon Art, London 1984.

The Year 1200: The Year 1200. I, The Exhibition, Catalogue by Konrad Hoffmann, 1970. II, A. Background Survey, 1970. – A Symposium, 1975.

Thoby: Paul Thoby: Le Crucifix, Nantes 1959.

Udf: L'Univers des Formes, cf. RO.

UdK: Universum d. Kunst.

Wesenberg: Rudolf Wesenberg: Frühe mittelalterliche Bildwerke, Düsseldorf 1972.

Wilson: David M. Wilson: Anglo-Saxon Art, London 1984.

Wrangel: Ewert Wrangel: Lunds Domkyrkas Konsthistoria, 1923.

ZDVK: Zeitschrift des Deutschen Vereins für Kunstwissenschaft.

Zeit d. Ottonen etc.: UdK: Die Zeit der Ottonen und Salier, von L. Grodecki, E. Mutherich, J. Taralon & F. Wormald, München 1973.

Årb. Aarbøger for nordisk Oldkyndighed og Historie.

NOTES *Noter*

(1) *NM*, inv.nr. D894, cf. note 159. Danish Art Treasures, London 1948, 51; *Oman*; *Schiller* 2, 124-25, 3, 484, Abb. 445; *NMD*, 92-93 (C.G. Schultz); *ERA*, 239 (nr. 229); *The Golden Age*, 204-06; *Marth*, 366; *Engemann*, 18. – (2) Rapporter i *NM*, cf. note 180. – (3) Åby krucifiks, *NM*, inv.nr. D629, cf. note 150 og 180; Odder krucifiks, *NM*, inv.nr. CCCCXXIII, cf. note 156, og Vellerupfigur, *NM*, inv.nr. D3771/1966, cf. note 203 og 207. – (4) Kerubkorset, *NM*, inv.nr. D23/1982, cf. note 158 og 180. – (5) *Schiller* 2, 110ff. – (6) Cf. note 175; *Gk* 23, 63-68 (»Cross-Type«). – (7) Cf. note 172. Kunst des Mittelalters in Sachsen. Festschrift Wolf Schubert, Weimar 1967, 237-46; *Haussherr* 131-68; *Schiller* 3, fig. 87. – (8) *OE* 2, 296-300. – (9) Skjern, Middelsom herred, cf. note 173 og 157; *Marth*, 376. – (10) Sindbjerg alter, *NM*, inv.nr. D927-28, cf. note 154; *Nørlund GA*, 6, 10; *Schiller* 3, 124-25, fig. 445. – (11) *Danmarks NM / NMD*, 92 (C.G. Schultz). – (12) Cf. note 180. – (13) Broddetorp alter, cf. note 160; Eriksbergskrin, cf. note 161. – (14) Jælaskrin, cf. note 162. – (15) Om Århus, som stedet hvorfra alter og skrin kan være kommet til Sverige, vil meddelelse blive givet andet steds. – (16) *Bloch*, 310-11 (Hannover 2150 »aus fast reinem Kupfer«); P.S. Professor Peter Bloch har venligt meddelt mig, at skemaet i *Staufer* V vil blive udvidet og revideret væsentligt i hans værk (om c. 650 bronzekrucifikser), der står over for udgivelse; det vil deraf fremgå, at krucifikser af næsten rent kobber findes i Bonn (Bloch II C 1, »Mittelitalien um 1130«), London, Victoria & Albert (Bloch V B 14, »Skandinavien 2. Hälfte 12.Jahrh.«) og Münster, Westf. Landesmus. (Bloch VII E 3 »Westfalen, 1. Hälfte 12.Jahrh.«). Ingen af dem tilhører Blochs Winchesterfolge »V A; Zeitschrift für Archäologie und Kunstgeschichte Bd. 42, 1985, 179; Maximilianmuseum zu Augsburg Inv. DM IX, 22 (»vergoldete Kupferguss«); Oevre maitresses du Musée, Liège 1980, 10-11 (»Cuivre coule? etc. – (17) Cf. note 5. – (18) *GB*, 4. – (19) *OE* 1, 423-424 (C 8), 2, 238-39 (Köln); *Hildesh. D*, 38-47; *UdK Zeit d. Ottonen etc.*, 92, fig. 82 (Reichenau), 104 (Corvey), 107 (før 1000), 1031, fig. 121 (Lorch), 133, fig. 125 (Trier, c. 984-85, en gentagelse af et Tours billede i Vivianbibelen udført 845-46 uden korsglorie af særtypen, hvad der peger i retning af, at typen er opstået mellem 945 og 985, cf. *Kahnsitz*, 79-82. I England forekommer den omkr. 1058-1076, *The Golden Age*, 78-79, cf. *Oman*, 384). – (20) Stavelot bibel, London, British Library, Add MS 28106 and 28107, *RiM*, 10-11 Colour plate II. Cf. *Marth* 62-71 (Liège) Abb. 1.

(21) *Tamdrup k.* (fig. 81); *Nørlund & Lind*, fig. 8, cf. fig. 24 (Hedensted), fig. 151 (Sindbjerg); *Mackeprang*, 172 (Anst kirke), 175 (Petersportalen, Slesvig). – (22) Odder, cf. note 156; Lisbjerg, cf. note 153; Stadil, cf. note 167; Broddetorp, cf. note 160; *Cinthio 1958* (Krucifix i Lund c. 1100, LUHM Cat.nr. 3704). Forgyldt bronzeamulet fundet 1976 på Revninge kirkegård ved Kerteminde (*NM* D1444/1977), *Arb*, 1976, 172; *Danefæ*, 7. – (23) Ornament, cf. note 89. – (24) *Gk*, 22-26, 64-65. – (25) Forbindelsen med det officielle England var stort set afbrudt, sålænge Vilhelm Erobreren levede, men derimod god med en personlighed som ærkebisp Anselm, da han var rejst fra England. Se i øvrigt s. 71 og L'idée de Nations dans l'Histoire de l'Europe par Henri Brugmans, Préface i Les Memoirs de l'Europe I, 1970. – (26) *Schlesw. Dom*, 145, 154. – (27) *Wesenberg*, 76, 106, Abb. 454 (Minden, 1060-70); *Swarzenski*, 57, Plate 104 (Helmarshausen, tidl. 12. årh.) cf. *Gk*, 85, note 86; *Hildesh. Dom*. – (28) *Wesenberg*, Abb. 103-104, 166-172 (St. Gallen, cf. *Merton*, Tafel 76 og 95,2), 374, 375. RO (*UdK Romanik* II), 174-75, fig. 143. (Om forholdet til Tours har Francois Avril venligt henvist mig til M. Schapiro: Two drawings in Auxerre, Studies in Art and Literature for Belle de Castra Greene, Princeton (New Jersey) Univ. Press 1954); cf.

Staufer II, 477 (Schwaben um 1130), 471 (Westfalen um 1130); *Staufer* V, 188 (Bloch, c. 1200), 192; – (29) *Nørlund GA*, 124. OE 1, 314-15 (Motivet findes i Ademar de Chabannes mønsterbog fra Limoges, 1000-1025). – (30) *Wesenberg*, Abb. 488, 491 (Minden); Rainer Kahnitz: Armillae aus dem Umkreis Friederich Barbarossa, Anzeiger des Germ. NM.s 1979, 21; *Staufer* V, Abb. 208 (Bloch, c. 1200). – (31) *Merton*, Tafel 76, 1-2; ZDVK 1941, 151-58 (Werden), cf. *Wesenberg*, Abb. 369-376, 354, 388, 445, 487; *Bloch*, Abb. 174, 175, 177, 181-183, 185-186, 192-195, 199, 202-203, 208-210, 212-213. – (32) *Wesenberg*, Abb. 376; *Bloch*, Abb. 210. – (33) *Bloch*, Abb. 190-191. – (34) *Bloch*, Abb. 177-179, 181-182, 192. – (35) *Staufer* II, 477-478. – (36) *Merton*, Tafel 76; *Wesenberg*, Abb. 218-219, 510; *Staufer* V, Abb. 181, 203. – (37) *DGC*, 87, ill. 107. – (38) *OE* 2, 246, 252. – (39) Susan La Niece har på British Museum foretaget en analyse af det mørke i graveringerne og konstateret, at det ikke var niello: »I found no evidence for niello in the engraving and the gilding runs into all the engraved lines. As the gilding would have been done after the niello, it would not be expected in the engraving if it had once held niello. I believe it is dirt, or wax«. *Oldeberg*, 60, 151, 222-28; *Nørlund GA* 2.ed 1968, 7-8*. Acta Archæologica Vol 53, 1982 (Kbh. 1983), 204 (Knud J. Krogh). – (40) *DGC*, 52, fig. 58 (Narbonne), fig. 61-62 og 77. – (41) *Bloch*, cf. *OE* 2, 391-95. – (42) *DGC*, 87, fig. 106. – (43) *OE* 1, 214 (Gero); cf. *Wesenberg* 11-16, 95; ZDVK 1941, 141-158 (Essen-Werden); cf. *Wesenberg*, 59; *Zeit d. Ottonen* etc., fig. 357. – (44) *RuM* I, 308, nr. J.34. – (45) *Wesenberg*, Abb. 367, 372 (St. Gallen Stiftsbibl. Codex 390/1, p. 27, Cod. 376, p. 191). – (46) London, British Library, MS Arundel 60, cf. *Oman*; *Zeit d. Ottonen etc.* (Francis Wormald) 253-55, fig. 259; *The Golden Age*, 82-83 (D.H. Turner) »The figure of Christ is highly stylised and recalls late eleventh-century Franco-Flemish miniature painting«, cf. *Kahsnitz*, 32-35 (»... die Lehrmeisterin westlicher Künstler (war) auch hier die byzantinische Kunst«). – (47) Cf. note 28. – (48) Broddetorp, cf. note 160. – (49) *DGC*, fig. 14. – (50) *DGC*, fig. 182.

– (51) RO (*UdK Romanik* II), 313. – (52) The Metropolitan Museum, New York, nr. 17.190.209. P.S. Professor Peter Bloch har venligt meddelt mig, at lændeklæder med zig-zagfolder helt som Lundøkorsets ikke er bemærket i Tyskland. – (53) Cf. note 44 (Frauenberg). Med en knude (knot) forstår jeg her noget, der buler ud, og det kan godt være en strop eller lidt af lændeklædet, der blot er trukket op og viser sig som en knude over bæltet, cf. de to »knuder« på siderne af lændeklædet på det skånske kors fra Ystad, fig. 40, Statens historiska Museum, Stockholm, *Marth*, 268-71. Nogle af de mange varianter Peter Bloch opregner i forbindelse med »Verknotung« (OE 2, 392-93) findes i Danmark og peger mod Tyskland. GLIM, cf. Nielsen, 22, fig. 3, Skånska Kloster, ed. E. Cinthio, Lund 1989 (Dalby-bogen). – (54) *Staufer* I, nr. 537, Abb. 327; *Kahnsitz*, 33, Abb. 34. – (55) *Nørlund GA*, 50. – (56) *Nørlund GA*, 51. – (57) *OE* 1, 200-201, 2, 253 (Trier Evangeliar af Gregor mester); cf. *Grimme*, 68. – (58) Cf. note 20 (Stavelot). – (59) Cf. note 46. – (60) *Gk*, 80. *Cinthio 1958*, fig. 3, baggrunden på Heggenfløjen i Oslo, på den forgyldte helgenskrinskantbort i Odense (cf. Fynske Studier XV, Odense bys Museer »Knuds-bogen« (Jens Vellev), Odense 1986), på Odderretablets Majestasbillede og Himmelfart (*DK*, Århus amt, 2540-41), på Lyngsjöfrontalet, og på Stavelot-retablet (Cluny, Paris c. 1150) har cirkler *uden* centerprik. Mønsteret forekommer som skulpturbaggrund på bronzestøbt arbejde (»Ewer for holy water«) fra Mainz, 1116-19, se *Swarzenski*, fig. 236, og som baggrund for ranker på en Provisur-Pyrix og korsfod fra Kloster Escherder, nu i Hildesheim (*Hildesh. D*, nr. 17, cf. *Springer*, kat. 28, K 244-253 (1150-75)). – (61) Cf. note 165; *Nørlund GA*, 178, fig. 158 (Mikael med *sværd*) cf. *SfV*, 20, fig. 22. – (62) *Nørlund & Lind*, fig. 126, fig. 128. – (63) *Oursel Rév*, 52-59, planche 19 (Civate S. Pietro al Monte), cf. Festschr. Werner Bornheim gen. Schilling 1980, 37 (Burgfelden); *Hil-*

desh. D, fig. 30 (Ratmann-M.). – (64) *Gk*, 35, 63, planche 22 (Starup), 24, fig. 25-26 (Onsbjerg), cf. *SfV*, 46 nr. 38. – (65) Cf. note 126. – (66) Cf. note 22 (Dalby). – (67) *DGC*, 50, fig. 55. – (68) *Wesenberg*, 13, 42 (Abb. 345), *Alexander*, 90, Pl. 16h). – (69) *Alexander*, 87-100; *Nyborg*; *SfV*, 37-39.

– (70) Paris, Bibl. Nationale, Latin 9448, cf. *Alexander*, 91, Pl. 19e. – (71) Legendaire de Citeaux IV, cf. *Oursel Cit.*, planche 35.

– (72) Paris, Bibl. Nationale, Latin 11685, fol 40; *Alexander*, 98, Pl. 19f. – (73) C.R. Dodwell: The Canterbury School of Illumination, Cambridge 1954, 26, 34, Pl. 21. – (74) Cf. note 69. – (75) *Wrangel*, 248-49; Den ikonografiske post 1973, nr. 3. – (76) Cf. note 63 (Civate: flere hoveder). – (77) *Wrangel*, 88, 304, fig. 277; G. Warner: A descriptive catalogue of illuminated MS in the library of C.W. Dyson Perrins, 1920, nr. 119, Pl. 108 (Bibel fra Justement ved Metz). – (78) Cf. note 186-87, *Lindahl* 8-11; *Guld i V*, 169-81; Studier tilegnet Otto Norn, 1990, 1-10; *Gk*, 85, note 76 og 85 (Korset har en forkert anbragt særform af Alfa-Omega). Vedr. dateringen cf. note 141 og 187. Om placeringen af slangen ved korsets fod se s. 30 og 40, cf. note 126, om indskriften note 187. – (79) *Lapière*, fig. 115 og 174; *Wilson*, fig. 143; *Wrangel*, 87-88, 304; *OE* 1, 252-54 (efter 1160); *Staufer II*, Abb. 517 (Weingarten um 1220). – (80) London, British Library, Add.Mss 14789, f. 83v, cf. front cover of *RiM*, cf. note 92. – (81) Manchester, John Rylands Library, cf. Studien zur Buchmalerei Festschr. K.H. Usener 1965, 145, fig. 5. – (82) ZDVK 1941, 6, 10 (A. Boeckler). – (83) *Wesenberg*, 80-88, Abb. 230-31, 253, 410, 499-500. – (84) *OE* 2, 253-54. – (85) Codex aureus epternacensis, Germanisches Nationalmuseum, Nürnberg, cf. *Kahsnitz*, Taf. 21-27.

– (86) *Oursel Cit.*, planche 35. – (87) *OE* 2, 295, E76 (c. 1140). – (88) Cf. note 83. – (89) *UdK Romanik I*, 229, Abb. 213 (Trier bogbind, »um 1100«), cf. *Steenbock*, kat. 79, Abb. 107; *Staufer*, II, 534. *Krüger*, 114, fig. 159, cf. *OE* 1, 445, c 20, 358-75 (Roger v. Helmarshausen – Theophilus). – (90) RO (*UdK Romanik II*), 312, cf. 93, fig. 76. – (91) Cf. note 20 (Stavelot); *RiM*, 10-12. – (92) Cf. note 80 (Park); *RiM*, 12-13; *RuM*, 372. – (93) Cf. note 81. – (94) Carl Nordenfalk: Celtic and Anglo-Saxon Painting, 1977; The Golden Age, 46-87; *Wrangel*, 81; *Wilson*; *Merton*, Tafel 89, 1-2, Tafel 94,1; J.J.G. Alexander: The decorated Letter, 1978. – (95) Cf. note 57, 103 og 146. – (96) *Kahsnitz*, 71f. – (97) *Lapière*, 179-81, fig. 172 (Bruxelles, B. R II 1639, fol. 6). – (98) Cf. note 80; *RuM* II, 372, fig. 15; *RiM*, 4, 12, Pl. 4. – (99) *OE* 1, 117-230. – (100) *OE* 1, 443-46 (c 20, Roger v. Helmarshausen). – (101) *OE* 1, 18-19. På Ludvig den Helliges psalter (Paris, Bibl. Nationale, Ms latin 10525) fol. 46, er der *malet* en ramme med hjørnekvadrater som Dalbybindets, *Grimme*, 148-150. – (102) Cf. note 153, 154, 163 (Agnus Dei), note 165-167 (Dove). – (103) *Grimme*, 56-57 (Farbtafeln 4 og 5), cf. note 146. En tegning i Auxerre (jfr. note 28) viser et lam i en medaljon placeret over en Christus majestas i mandorla. Lammet tilbedes af de 24 ældste. Tegningen stammer fra Tours, der var et center i Karolingernes rige. –

(104) Cf. note 198. Fritze Lindahl i MIV, 5, 1975, 52-55; *SfV*, 44, nr. 33, cf. ZDVK, 1941, fig. 72 (Lam 1226). Lam på danske mønter siden Knud den Stores tid. – (105) Cf. note 154. – (106) Cf. note 153. – (107) Dansk Kunsthistorie I, 55 (Externstein). Cf.74 *Swarzenski*, fig. 289: Lambert's Soul carried to Heaven (Saint-Bertin 1125-50). – (108) *OE* 2, 428-37 (»die Gruppe der gestichelten Elfenbeine«), *DGC*, 102F, *UdK*, Romanische Kunst I, 26of (omkr. 1150). – (109) Cf. note 151 og 153. – (110) Cf. note 151. – (111) Ornamenter, se fig. 5, 9, og 10, cf. *Marth*, fig. 49 (Ystad) bagsiden, cf. note 53. – (112) *Blindheim*. – (113) Lionello Venturi: George Rouault, New York 1940, (Paris 1948). – (114) *Danmarks NM / NMD*, 92, cf. *Gk*, 17, 61, note 30. Det synes klart, at indskrifterne på Gunhildkorsets for- og bagside hører til korsets »program«, medens indskrifterne på de andre sider er problematiske for alle, der er

opmærksomme på, at indskrifter på genstande ofte er *senere* tilføjelser. – (115) Det indledende R i tredie linie synes at erstatte et C. Det klassiske, kantede E bruges – som på Lisbjergalteret – sammen med den krumme form. Om farvestof, se note 39. – (116) *Nørlund GA*, 23. – (117) Hullerne anes på fig. 2 og er markeret på fig. 10. – (118) Beretninger i *NM*. Gunnar Knudsen og Marius Kristensen: Danmarks gamle Personnavne I, 1939-40 (»Atlmar« stikord for Almar, Almarus. Der henvises til oldtysk Athalmar Almar). *NM* kataloger 1911, 1917 og 1920 har Altmar (montre 568). – (119) *Nørlund GA*, 55-56, cf. *Gk*, fig. 36 (Ribe Tympanon fra c. 1140). – (120) Seneste læsning og oversættelse til dansk i notat (*NM*) af Marie Stoklund, som jeg takker for bistand med dette afsnit. Den engelske oversættelse efter *Oman*, 384. – (121) Cf. note 118 og 120 (*Oman*). Bo Seltén: The Anglo-Saxon Heritage in Middle English Personal Names, East Anglia 1100-1399 II (Lund), 30.

– (122) At ærkebispen forbyder salg til private af kirkelige billeder på torvet i Lund viser, at et sådant salg har fundet sted. Armen af et bronzekrucifiks er fundet ved udgravning af middelalderborgen på Clausholm (HL: Clausholms Bygningshistorie 1958, 14, fig. 8). – (123) Hugo Matthiessen: Limfjorden, 1936, 33. På Joh. Meyers kort (c. 1650) er Lundø endnu en ø, på Videnskabernes Selskabs kort (1789) er Lundø landfast med Jylland.

– (124) Kerubkorsets tap er 14,5 cm lang, *Gk*, fig. 12. – (125) Se s. 30 (om lansen som våben mod dragen) og *Nørlund GA*, 12-13, cf. *Springer*, 131-32 (1130-40) og Arb. 1984, 101-112 (Marie Stoklund om gravkors). – (126) Cf. note 78; *Gk*, fig. 78; *Marth*, 43-45; *Wesenberg*, Abb. 267, 269-271, 288, 312, 392, 393; *Engemann*, 18, 30. – (127) Cf. *Gk*, 81, note 36. »Korsets hyldning« finder sted hvert år under den katolske kirkes Langfredags-liturgi. Venligt meddelt af biskop Hans I. Martensen. På fotografiet fig. 2 er en forgyldt kopi af Lundøkorset holdt frem sådan, som forfatteren erindrer at have oplevet det i Orvieto Langfredag d. 7. april 1939. – (128) Danish Art Treasures, Catalogue London 1948, No. 107. – (129) *Oman*. – (130) The Golden Age, No 75, 90-92, colourplate 23; *Wilson*, 190, fig. 240 (»The Drahmal Cross«, Bruce Dickins & Alan S.C. Ross: The Dream of the Rood, 13-16 (»The Brussels Cross«), Michel Alexander: The Earliest English Poems 1982, 103-110. – (131) *Oman*. – (132) Cf. note 130, Dickins & Ross, 16. – (133) *Steenstrup III*, 342. – (134) *Steenstrup III*, 339-40. – (135) *Schlesw. Dom*, 145, 154. – (136) Oscar Karpa: Die Kirche St. Michaelis zu Hildesheim, cf. *Hildesh. D*, og V.H. Elbern: Dom und Domschatz in Hildesheim, 1979. – (137) V. Lorenzen: Benediktinerklostre 1933, 144ff; *Steenstrup III*, 249. Knud den Store kom på fredelig fod med Bremen i forbindelse med sin rejse til Tyskland. – (138) Nyt fra *NM*, dec. 1984, nr. 25, 13 (Elisabeth Munksgaard). – (139) *Minden*, 16, 51; cf. Kunst und Kultur im Weserraum 2 (1967), 565-66, nr. 244. – (140) Cf. note 26; *Schlesw. Dom*, 142. – (141) Cf. note 78. Årstal 1141

81. *Tamdrup. Rester af kalkmaleri fra c. 1120. Konturen af den korsfæstedes hoved ses med korsglorie som baggrund. To mænd slår nagler gennem den korsfæstedes hænder.*

82. Tamdrupkalken.

usikkert, nogle mener 1143, cf. Dansk biografisk Leksikon og *Skyum-N.* – (142) Cf. note 152 og 199. – (143) Cf. note 197 og 199. – (144) *Cinthio*, 107. – (145) Cf. note 152 og 199. – (146) Cf. note 103, 104, 193, 194, 198. – (147) *Fests. HL* (Fritze Lindahl: Haraldsborgskatten).

(148) Tamdrup-kalk, *GB*, 27, *Bæksted*, 36. Det kan ikke godtgøres, at *ornamentstrimlerne* fra Tamdrup har hørt til samme arbejde som pladerne, cf. *Nørlund GA.* (Tamdrup-plader *NM*, inv.nr. D801). –

(149) *Nørlund GA*, tavle VI; cf. Danmarks Riges Historie, I, 363 (Joh. Steenstrup om Harald Blåtand). *Årb.*, 1968, De gyldne Altre I, Tamdrup (Den viste rekonstruktion umuliggøres af de bevarede pladers mål). *GB*, 5, 10, 26-29, Tvl. 11-12; *Tamdrup k.*, 71ff. (Inger-Lise Kolstrup; den som fig. 4 viste gengivelse er Nørlunds fra 1926. NMs opsætning blev ændret 1979-80. At ændringen af »dåbspladen« ikke er en rettelse, foretaget af rent tekniske grunde, er bekræftet af konservator Karen Stemann Petersen i notat af 8.10.1979.

– (150) Åbykrucifikset, *NM*, inv.nr. D629, cf. note 3. *Nørlund GA*, 225-26, *DBhg* 45-51 (c. 1100), *Danmarks NM / NMD*, 84-85, *Gb*, 11, *DK*, Århus amt, bd. 3, 1442-44. Træfigur, formentlig fra 11. årh., men i 12. årh. beklædt med kobber og forgyldt. Til træfigurens flade baghoved har rimeligvis hørt en korsglorie. Issen er omdannet med et tilføjet stykke træ, hvortil kronen er tilføjet (fig.83), cf. Lisbjergalterets krucifiks, der formentlig har haft en tilsvarende træforøgelse med krone (*Nørlund GA*, 225-26). –

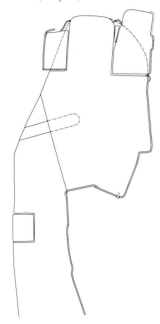

83. *Åbyfigurens hoved med issens oprindelige kontur vist med punkteret linie. Bag halsen ses et snit af det lange stykke træ begge arme er skåret i.*

(151) Tirstrupkrucifikset. *Nørlund GA*, 100-102, 230 (»1150-75«), og 52-53 (c. 1175), *Danmarks NM / NMD* 90-91, *GB* tavle 14, *Gk*, 25, note 63, 86-87 (farvespor, cf. notater i *NM*.s arkiv). *Swarzenski*, Tab. 109 (»1140«). Træfiguren har været malet, før den blev kobberbeklædt. Sammenholdes i »profil« med Vellerup krucifiks af Nørlund (*DBhg*, 53). Trækærnen i korsstammen er forkortet og metalpladerne forskudt i forholdet til figuren.

(152) Odenseskrin, cf. note 60 og note 199. At dele af skrinenes metaldekoration kan være fra omkr. 1140, noteres her som en mulighed, der undersøges, cf. note 199. – (153) Lisbjergalteret, *NM*, inv.nr. D287. *Nørlund GA*, 227-230 (eng.), Tavle 1-2, og *DBhg* (c. 1150). *Danmarks NM / NMD*, 88-89; *GB*, 2-3, 7, 12, 15, 22, Tavle 23; *DK*, Århus amt, bd. 3, 1400-1412, »o. 1150(-1200)«. *Lasco* (Pl. 169 »1140«). *Gk*, 85, note 85. Lisbjergalterets krucifiks, cf. note 151, 11. årh. Kobberbeklædning fra omkr. 1140. Det øverste af hovedets trækerne omdannet til tap, som den, der går op i Åbykrucifiksets kronepart, cf. note 150. – (154) Sindbjergalteret, *NM*, inv.nr. D927-28, cf. note 10, *Nørlund GA*, 238-241, 50 (plade med lam stjålet, cf. note 167). *GB*, 6, 10, Tavle 10. – (155) Orøkorset. For- og bagsideplader, cf. note 78 og 187. – (156) Odderretabel med krucifiks, *NM*, inv.nr. CCCCXXIII. *Nørlund GA*, 231-34, *GB*, 9, 23, Tavle 13, *DK*, Århus amt, 2536-2551 (»o. 1150-75«). – (157) Skjernkorset, Skjern kirke, cf. note 9 og 173; *Trap:Danmark*, Viborg amt, Bd. 17, 391; *Marth*, 376. – (158) Kerubkorset, *NM*, inv.nr. D23/1982, cf. note 4 og 180 (metalanalyser). – (159) Lundøkorset, *NM*, inv.nr. D894. Note 1 (fremmedsproget lit.) note 179 (nordisk lit.) note 180 (metalanalyser). – (160) Broddetorpalter, Stockholm, Statens historiska museum. *Nørlund GA*, 230-31. – (161) Eriksbergskrin, Stockholm, Statens historiska museum. *Nørlund GA*, 116-18. De »udstikkende« fødder er næppe oprindelige og kendes vist ikke fra den tidlige middelalder, sml. *Liebgott*, 115. – (162) Jälaskrin, Skara, Skaraborgs Länsmuseum; *Nørlund GA*, 18; Ernst Fischer: Västergötlands kürkliga Konst under Medeltiden, Uppsala, 135-137. Meget lig Eriksbergskrinet og med tilsvarende fødder, der peger i retning af, at de to skrin en tid har hørt sammen. – (163) Ølstfrontalet, *NM*, inv.nr. D5144; *Nørlund GA*, 234-237. *DBhg*, 55 (»1200-1225«); *L'Europe Gothique XIIᵉ – XIVᵉ siècles*, Paris 1968, nr. 397, fig. 100. *Lasco*, fig. 285 (»1150-1160«) »Korsfæstelsen« følger nøje det billedskema, *Kahsnitz*, 32-35, har fulgt fra Byzans til Köln (»um 1150«) og Maasområdet, cf. note 46. – (164) Kuml 1958, 1959, 9-20; *Skyum-N*, 121; *Gk*, 90, note 155. – (165) Sahlalteret, Sahl kirke, *Nørlund GA*, 241-245; *GB*, 19; O. Norn and S. Skovgaard Jensen: The House of Wisdom, 1990; *SfV*, 20. – (166) Odderfrontalet, *NM*, inv.nr. CCCCXXIII. *Nørlund GA*, 234-37; *SfV*, 15, 24-25 (o. 1225): *GB*, Tavle 4-6; *DK* Aarhus amt 2536-2551, 2588. – (167) Stadilfrontalet, Stadil kirke, Ringkøbing amt. *Nørlund GA*, 5, 121, 243-45. 2. ed. 8*. Gudslam nyere kopi efter Sindbjergalter. *GB*, 9, Tavle 4-6. *SfV*, 24-25 (o. 1235). – (168) I behandlingen af bogmaleriet fra Citeaux noterer Oursel, at flere af de høje, slanke figurer peger hen mod senere fransk portalskulptur, og i omtalen af Frauenberger krucifikset (cf. note 44) beklages det, at forholdet mellem Köln og Frankrig endnu ikke er udredt. I 1983 gøres der op med det urimelige i at klassificere skulpturer fra omkr. 1140 som gotiske eller romanske (*RO*, 100-102). – (170) Korrespondance i *NM*. – (171) Fotografier i *NM*. – (172) Cf. note 158 (Kerubkors) og note 7 og 8 om »kerub« og »seraf«. *Beckett I*, 216, betegner de to figurer, der flankerer Lisbjerg-madonnaen som »en kerub og en seraf«, medens *Nørlund GA*, 74, siger »keruber og serafer«. De to englelignende figurer, der på Dalbybogen viser hænder på kerubmaner (Ez 10, 8 og 12) og ikke står på hjul, kalder *Nielsen*, 22, »keruber«, cf. *Arb* 1983, 185. – (173) Cf. note 9 og 157; *Marth*, 376 (»Seraph«). – (174) Om det 19. århundredes grovsortering af alle middelalder-frembringelser i »romanske« og »gotiske« cf. HL: Danmarks Bygningskultur II (1955), 242-46. Når Beckett 1927 anbringer Vel-

lerupkrucifikset i sit bind om »Gotiken« – med henvisning til fransk plastik, må Nørlund 1950 præcisere, at det drejer sig om den »fransk-romanske stil«, cf. note 168, 203 og 207. – (175) Cf. note 6; *Marth* skelner mellem »skånske« og danske kors. – (176) Kataloger i *NM*. – (177) *Oman.* – (178) *Oman.* – (179) Trap: Danmark 1962, E. Horskjær: »o. 1200-1250«. Tage E. Christiansens reviderede katalogtekst *NM* 1972: »1025-1075«. – (180) Rapporter i *NM*.s arkiv fra William Larsen, Birthe Gottlieb, Peter Henrichsen og J.C. Balling Jensen. – (181) *ZDVK* 1941 (Essen Werden Krucifix) *Bloch*, 310-11 (*Staufer Bronzekrucifixer*), *Oldeberg* (Krucifikser i Statens historiska museum) er blandt de relativt få, der er undersøgt, cf. note 16. – (182) *RIM*, 8, farvetavle I. Francois Avril daterer 1983 billedet til 1130-40 (*RO*, 213). – (183) Cf. note 153. – (184) Cf. note 154; Hikuin 1, 84 (Moltke). – (185) *Nørlund GA*, 225; Hikuin 1, 84. – (186) Cf. note 78, 154 og 155; *Bæksted*, 36; Hikuin 1, 85-86, note 15 (Moltke); *Guld i V.*, 178. – (187) *Krüger*, 164, 176; cf. *GLIM.* – (188) Cf. note 80. – (189) *Nørlund GA*, 206. Ud over reliefpladerne har *NM* fra Tamdrup noget glat, ornamenteret metal. Det spiller en rolle for Nørlunds datering, men behøver ikke oprindelig at have hørt sammen med reliefferne. – (190) *Nørlund GA*, 174. Knudsbogen, 190 og 195. – (191) Tamdrup kan tænkes at høre til det gods, Erik Emune menes at have beslaglagt efter Magnus og Niels (*Skyum-N*, 137). Magnus Nielsens enke, Richiza kan måske også komme i betragtning. Mandspersonen kan i så fald være den Knud, der kronedes i Viborg 1157. Hun var datter af den svenske kong Sverker og blev – uvist hvornår – gift med en russisk fyrst Volodar efter 1134, hvor Magnus faldt ved Fodevig. – (192) *Gb*, 28-29; *Skyum-N*, 88. *Tamdrup k.*, 77-78 (Inger-Lise Kolstrup). – (193) *Skyum N*, 81. – (194) *Skyum-N*, 85; *Gk*, 54-55 (Ribe domkirke som »imperial« gravkirke). – (195) Hafnia nr. 8 1981, 101ff. (Søren Kaspersen om *David*); *Rom. St.* 4, 133-54 (Inger-Lise Kolstrup om jyske granitrelieffer). Den velsignende hånd har måske en forklaring, der hænger sammen med at kongen var gået i kloster 1146. Figurerne må i så fald være fra denne tid. – (196) *Cinthio*, 127-29; samme: Lunds Domkyrka 1953. 8. 48-59. – (197) *Nørlund GA*, 50 (Lam på altre). Når så mange korslam-medailloner er fundet i Nørrejylland, kan man gætte på, at en del »Erikianere« efter det endelige nederlag på Grathe Hede har fundet det bedst at skille sig af med »emblemet« (cf. note 200). Lise Bertelsen har venligt meddelt mig, at næsten alle korslam-medailloner er nørrejyske jordfund. En afhandling derom »Præsentation af Ålborggruppen, en gruppe dyrefibulaer uden dyreslyng« vil hun publicere i *Årb*. Om »Jellingløven« som »kongemærke« se Fritze Lindahl i Historisk Årbog fra Roskilde Amt 1982, 36-43. Om Herman, cf. note 143 og 199; Dansk Biografisk Leksikon (Ellen Jørgensen). Han kom fra Rolduck v. Aachen. Hall Koch: Kongemagt og Kirke, 1963, 184-85, cf. *Skyum-N*, se reg.

(198) *NM*, inv.nr. D8361, cf. note 104 og 146. Erik Klippings korslam er indgraveret i en sten (blodjaspis), som man mente var Golgatha, og er rimeligvis et italiensk arbejde. Når man erindrer, at paven sendte dronning Margrethe I et personligt sekret til brug på breve, hun sendte ham, kan man spørge, om ikke stenen fra Viborg er en gave fra paven – måske til Erik Ejegod. Den kan godt være fra omkr. 1100. Tilnavnet »Lam« kan måske være tvetydigt, cf. *Skyum-N*, 77 (om Erik Emune). Saxo (14. bog) siger i Winkel Horns oversættelse, 95, at Erik Lam fik tilnavnet på grund af sin tålmodighed. A. Hvitfeld (Folieudg. I, 102-03) siger det var »for hans simpelheds skyld«, medens Holberg I (1753) hævder, det »var i henseende til hans enfoldighed«. – (199) Arild Hvitfeld, Folieudg. I, 103: Ved Odense Klosterets ophøjelse (til en slags »rigskloster«) 1140 medvirkede Erik Lam personligt tilligemed »Bisp Herman af Slesvig«. Når der i kirken er passet på to »helgenskrin« må man spørge, om det ene ikke i virkeligheden var Erik Lams kiste. – (200) *Gk*, 44. Skal man tro Bayeux-tapetet, har Vilhelm Erobreren haft et kors som felttegn i fanedugen, *ERA*, 80. Ribe-Ulf førte Svend Grathes fane i

84. *Lundøkorset og Kerubkorset fotograferet på Nationalmuseet 1931.*

kampen på Grathe Hede, men om fanemærket forlyder der intet. Erik Lams søn – og med ham utvivlsomt talrige »Erikianere« – kæmpede på Svends side. Det peger i retning af, at lammets »store tid« endte 1157, cf. note 197. – (201) Cf. note 108. – (202) *Nørlund GA*, 205. – (203) *Beckett* II, 121-23. –

(204) *NM*, Naturvidenskabelig afd. (NNU) A 6588 (22. dec. 1988 ved Kjeld Christensen (Vellerupfiguren fig. 23-25)). – (205) Skrivelse af 8. jan. 1992 fra Niels Bonde, (NNU). – (206) *Nørlund GA*, 7. Rapport nr. 18, 1991 fra NNU ved Niels Bonde, *NM*. – (207) *Beckett* II, 123, *DBhg*, 54. – (208) Det er kun i fantasien, vi kan se en sådan mester på farten! Hvem – og hvor mange – der har været med til at formidle forbindelsen mellem øst og vest – og med det store udland, kan vi ikke sige noget om. Når der i det foregående tales om Lundøkorsets mester og Kerubkorsets, drejer det sig om folk, hvis eksistens vi alene kender fra de to kors.

85. *Valdemar den Stores korsbannermønt (2/1).*

INDEX

80